CRIMINAL THINKING REFORM

I0092904

Perrion Roberts

www.TrueVinePublishing.org

Criminal Thinking Reform
Perrion Roberts

Published by
True Vine Publishing Co.
810 Dominican Dr. Ste. 103
Nashville, TN 37228
www.TrueVinePublishing.org

ISBN: 978-1-956469-68-4 Paperback
ISBN: 978-1-956469-69-1 eBook

Cover design by Perrion Roberts

Printed in the United States of America.

----CONFIDENTIALITY----

Do not write anything you wish to keep private in this book.

Table of Contents

About Criminal Thinking Reform

This workbook is designed specifically to help inmates and formally incarcerated inmates live a crime-free life by changing their criminal thinking to responsible thinking. It can be used as a class text and as a reference guide for inmates to use outside of class.

It's also a systematic, cognitive-behavioral, step-by-step treatment strategy designed to enhance self-image, promote positive, productive identity, and facilitate the development of higher stages of moral reasoning.

This program will help participants significantly increase moral reasoning levels, enhance life purpose, facilitate increased social support, and gives participants more perceived control over their lives. Participants must implement daily the steps designed in this workbook to change their conscious decision-making to a higher level of rational thinking.

By following this guideline, a participant will have a significantly lower rearrest and reincarceration level. This workbook is also designed for a participant who has been released from prison for more than 10 years.

This workbook is to help participants exercise the skills that were introduced in that chapter. In addition, each chapter in the workbook includes fill-in-the-blank examples for participants to answer. Finally, there are blank pages at the end of the book on which the participants can write notes. For some participants, this workbook will serve as the main text for research and writing courses that they must complete within their prison sentence.

There are group exercises included at the end of each chapter. This workbook will be used as an ancillary to the main text for other participants. In this case, the instructor will incorporate one or more of the chapters from this workbook into their regular course content to teach specific criminal thinking exercising skills. Because the instructor might teach only specific chapters, they will tell the participant which handouts and which chapter to use.

Chapter 1
Criminal Thinking and Behavior

"To have once been a criminal is no disgrace. To remain a criminal is the disgrace."

-Malcolm X

Why do people commit criminal acts?

Are they pure evil in nature?

What compels people to behave in criminal ways is a concern for many criminologists and psychologists. Unfortunately, lawmakers and policymakers attempt to understand this behavior as a whole when it simply boils down to one person.

The reason why you are engaging in criminal behaviors is specific to you. The ramifications of those actions are also specific to you. **So, it is you who must change and become better.** All of your actions are caused by your criminal thinking, and those thoughts are consistent patterns of distorted thinking errors that result in irresponsible and arrestable behavior. One of the most common errors in thinking is the failure to consider the injury to others. As a general rule, criminal thinkers do not consider the effect of their actions on others. Several criminals have a history of antisocial behavior. At the same time, others suffer from antisocial/pro-criminal (attitudes and values), pro-criminal associates and isolation from others who are anti-criminals, temperamental and personality factors, including psychopathy, impulsivity, and other cognitive deficits.

Recovery is tough. It is painful, bitter, and disquieting. Recovery can be nerve-racking, whether you struggle with addiction, risky behaviors, or getting in trouble with the law. It will take every bone in your body, every muscle, every tissue, and nerve fiber to say no to things you would previously do in the blink of an eye. It will take more than just time and energy to break this cycle. It will soak all your energy and drain you until you see some positive results. **Trust the process.**

There are plenty of steps to recovery, but the first and most important step is to take responsibility for your mistakes and accept the consequences of your behavior. Since the first step is self-reflection, you need to sit in a quiet place and think about your life honestly and truthfully. If you're not ready to confront your deepest thoughts and criminal behavior, this workbook will be difficult for you because that is just the beginning.

Fact Finder: *"Criminal thinking is a consistent pattern of distorted thinking errors resulting in irresponsible and arrestable behavior. One of the most common errors in criminal thinking is the failure to consider the injury to others. As a general rule, criminal thinkers do not consider the effect of their actions."*

The National Institute of Corrections developed Thinking for a Change (T4C), a cognitive-behavioral curriculum that concentrates on changing the criminogenic thinking of offenders. There are National Institutes all over the country trying to figure out how to help a criminal change the way they think. Do you believe that you can change your thinking patterns? Yes, there is a way out of that trap called the cognitive treatment of offenders. With effort and practice, even the most violent offenders can learn to change their thinking about other people and themselves. Most importantly, you will learn to be good and feel good about it.

Changing your habits can be difficult and painful for you, especially if you are unwilling to let go of criminal thinking and behavior. The path to recovery is, albeit challenging, but it is rewarding. Because at the end of the day, you get to change how your life turns out. Consistent baby steps will help you get to the end of the road. So, you have the power to say,

"This is not how my story will end."

There are many factors in your life as an offender directly related to recidivism called criminogenic. Research has identified six factors directly related to crime: low self-control, anti-social personality, anti-social values, criminal peers, substance abuse, and dysfunctional family.

Most people like yourself who have criminal-like thinking and behavior find it difficult to break the cycle, and the road to recovery will be even tougher for them. A way to recognize your criminal-like behavior is by playing a game. It's called the *"criminal game,"* A.K.A *"Con Game."* Once you have been able to play the game, you will be able to identify the areas of your life that this game has influenced. Then, you can start working on yourself and make a conscious effort not to repeat the game.

To recover, you have to break this cycle and get to the path of recovery, breaking from whatever is causing your addictive behavior and your criminal acts. If you are struggling with this, this workbook will be very helpful for you. It will help you identify your faulty thought processes and motivate you to modify your actions. Although, you have to be faithful to yourself and take responsibility for your actions instead of playing the blame game.

The decisions you make and what choices your behavior influences are all determined by your brain. Inside you is a person that is full of talent and potential. You are full of capabilities and qualities that are unique and specific to you. They make you special. If you look deep down, you will realize that you have a force inside you that constantly pushes you to achieve your dreams and goals, determine your destiny, fulfill your dreams, and that you're on the road to having a good life.

There are many aspects of our personality hidden inside of us. Ones that want to make things right want to stop hurting others and themselves by doing drugs, engaging in theft, robbery, and reckless behavior. However, the past can be difficult to move on from. Every time you try to change, you find something within you stopping you or telling you that you will never be the same no matter what you do.

(Try thinking of this)

"Don't try to be perfect. Try to be better. If you made a mistake, learn from it. Move on. You're already one step ahead of your past."

Q1.) What are criminal thinking errors?

_____

_____

_____

_____

Q2.) What are criminal thinking patterns?

_____

_____

_____

_____

Q3.) Can criminal thinking patterns among known offenders be changed? ___ Yes ___ No. Explain.

_____

_____

_____

_____

Q4.) What is "Thinking for a Change"?

_____

_____

_____

_____

Q5.) Now, did you ever play the *'criminal game?'*
___Yes ___ No. Elaborate on your answer.

_____

_____

_____

Q6.) How, why, and who did you hurt in the process? Take an extra paper if required, but truthfully write down what you have done in the past or present.

_____

_____

_____

_____

Q7.) What do you think about yourself and your behavior?

_____

_____

_____

_____

Now is the time you must be completely honest about yourself and your choices. Write down all of your past criminal behavior. It is pointless to lie to yourself. Explain who did you hurt and why. The extra paper will be required.

Do you love yourself? If so, what is your plan to change your criminal thinking behavior to achieve total self-love?

Group Activity

You don't have to be alone in the process of recovery. You can be a part of a group or share it with a friend.

Your first task is to attend an imaginary person's funeral. Appoint a mediator in your room who'll be mediating this activity. The words the mediator will say are marked in bold.

"This person shares your life story but isn't exactly you. You are supposed to view your life from a third person's perspective and think about what people say. Instead, you'll be an attendee to the funeral who will have to give an opinion about this person's life. You will share your opinion with us. View your life in retrospect and the choices you made."

Now, is anyone willing to volunteer?

Give each person 2 minutes to brainstorm their response and 3 minutes to say those words aloud to the group. Move order wisely and make sure everyone in the room visits their funeral.

E.g., *He was a lost cause. He always got in trouble. His wife and children suffered a lot because of him.*

Now, each person in the room will share how they think people will react to their deaths and the kind of words they'll use.

So, the first question is, are you satisfied with what you think people will say about you?

Give 2-3 participants a chance to answer.

Now, after imagining the kind of things people will say about you, don't you think you could have changed that? Does the thought that people will not even bother to show up when you die to compel you to think it's time to change your behavior?

Give a few participants a chance to answer these questions.

Is this how you want your life to end?

After a moment of silence, say,

"What you just saw might be your future unless you decide to change your present."

Chapter 2

A Difficult Path, but Worth the Effort

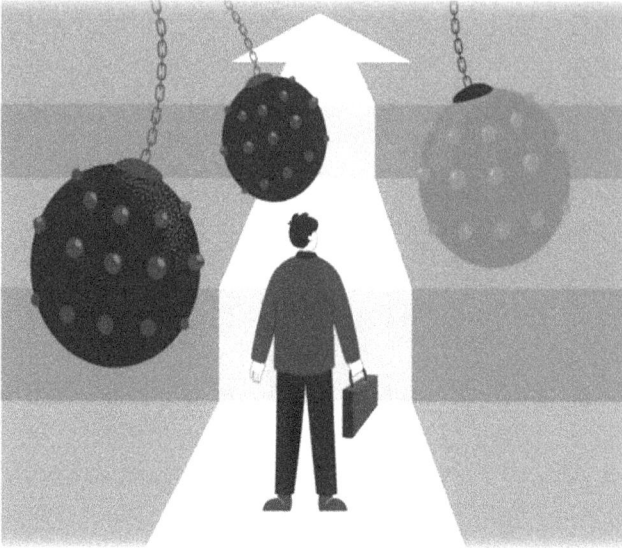

"In the middle of every difficulty lies an opportunity."
-Albert Einstein

As we have established in the first chapter, the road to recovery starts with self-reflection and responsibility for your actions, aspiring for a better life. You must first take ownership of your actions and thinking. Since you are out to change your life, it may seem overwhelming, and you may find yourself confused about where you should start.

To answer the question, *'Where Do I Start?'* you must start from your current situation. Your past mistakes may make it difficult to think of your present, but you must change your current thinking to have a better future. You have a chance not to repeat the shortcomings of your past and become so well-behaved that your past misdemeanors can be forgotten.

"I'm Not Telling You It Is Going to Be Easy; I'm Telling You It's Going to Be Worth It."

It takes small steps to make a big change in your life. You don't need to change how you live or change your name, or move to a new country to modify your life. You need to walk a path that is difficult but greatly rewarding. Start small, take baby steps at first, pick up the pace and start running toward a better life when you are good at it.

First of all, to narrow down your self-reflection process, start by listing three criminal thought processes or behaviors that you no longer wish to continue. These three criminal beliefs will not be a part of the new you, and your journey toward recovery starts with parting ways with them.

Criminal Thinking Reform Workbook

List three criminal beliefs or behaviors that you wish to leave behind.

- _____
_____
_____

- _____
_____
_____

- _____
_____
_____

Your reflections or thinking before starting this activity should be this way.

> **"I have spent my life recklessly. I have shown no regard for the laws and rules made by a civilized society. I have made no progress as an individual and have always blamed other people or found reasons to make exceptions for myself."**
>
> *-Perrion Roberts*

> **"** *I now understand that I am not exempt from the rules. I am a member of this society like every other person. The decisions I make, the activities I partake in influence my life. My actions have consequences, and I must accept full responsibility.* **"**
>
> *-Perrion Roberts*

> **"** *I have acted like a helpless victim throughout my life and blamed my family members, situations, or circumstances for my behavior, and it has led me nowhere. But, I now know that good things will only happen to me if I am willing to change myself and take full responsibility for my actions.* **"**
>
> *-Perrion Roberts*

Even though these sentences may just appear as words, even for just being words, they are powerful ones. What these words do, they no longer make you an exception or give excuses for breaking the rules. It puts you on the same pedestal as everyone else. You are not the only one who had a tough life or grew up having nothing.

There were plenty of men and women before you who faced the same kind of adversity. Instead of succumbing to the pressure on the streets, they became extraordinary men and women like Judge Greg Mathis, Curtis 50 Cent Jackson, Steve Jobs, Bill

Gates, Oprah Winfrey, Tyler Perry, Dolly Parton, and Howard Schultz, just to name a few.

Today, you need to confront the criminal in you. It's a time-out for your reckless actions. Now it's time to stop playing the criminal game. You will not simply act out of desperation or be shoved around like a football. You will now make your way and live life according to your own set of desires. You can decide how the rest of your life will be. So, you decide, will it be prison or someplace meaningful and peaceful?

Your journey as a recovering addict or criminal will be tough and challenging. You need to work on a couple of things to change your behavior—the first is developing self-control. To develop self-control, you first need to understand the concept of it. Two famous criminologists, Michael Gottfredson and Travis Hirschi, proposed the theory of self-control in Gottfredson's book *'A General Theory of Crime (1990).'* According to them, the very reason a crime is committed is to serve a person's self-interest. They define self-control as *"the ability to forego immediate or near-term pleasures that have some negative consequences and to the ability to act in favor of longer-term interests."*

So, to practice self-control, you must engage in deferred or delayed gratification. Immediate or constant gratification is a determinant of deviant or criminal behavior. As the theory suggests, criminals engage in risky behaviors that seem to work out for them at the moment. They seldom think of their behaviors' long-term consequences on their lives.

Delayed or deferred gratification refers to resisting the temptation to receive prompt pleasure or happiness for long-term benefit. For example, shoplifting will give you the pleasure of getting a sparkly and dangly accessory for the moment. But in the long run, if you are caught, you will have to suffer the consequences. Learning delayed gratification will teach you how to develop self-control and stop you from making bad choices.

Another important part of changing yourself or modifying your behavior is accepting that you are the captain of your own ship. You are responsible for what happens to you. The psychology of the blame game revolves around the concept of shame and guilt. People play the blame game because they are too hesitant to feel guilty for what they have done. To avoid feeling worthless and shameful, they find it easier to blame others than feel guilty about themselves.

So, you must avoid blaming people around you, like your dysfunctional family or your circumstances, and start acting like responsible individuals. Constantly remind yourself that there have been people in the past who made sure to rise above their situations and become extraordinary and exceptional people.

In his book, '7 Habits of Highly Effective People,' Stephen R. Covey describes effective people as proactive and not reactive. Reactive people seek other people to blame when faced with trouble or difficulties. Proactive people are not an outcome of their circumstances; they make solutions out of problems as they go.

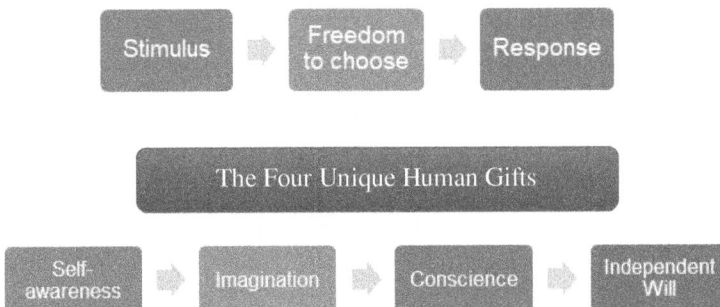

Stimulus	⇨	Freedom to choose	⇨	Response

The Four Unique Human Gifts

Self-awareness	⇨	Imagination	⇨	Conscience	⇨	Independent Will

The flowchart above shows that when people are faced with troubling situations, they can make choices based on four unique human gifts. You don't necessarily have to take on a negative or criminal path. If you have previously not followed this path, take this as a future guideline.

"I am not a product of my circumstances. I am a product of my decisions."

-Stephen R.Covey

No matter how competent a person is, they will not have sustained and lasting success unless they can effectively lead themselves, influence, engage and collaborate with others and continuously improve and renew their capabilities. These elements are at the heart of personal, team, and organizational effectiveness.

Moving from a path of criminal thinking and behavior to more responsible thinking will require overcoming obstacles. You will encounter setbacks and troubling circumstances. You have to take it upon yourself to abstain from acting out without thinking and have to think things through before you make a choice.

As you move away from the criminal game, you get closer and closer to changing your life. By constantly making informed choices, you will simply defeat the criminal game. However, if you repeatedly beat the criminal game, you will no longer play it and become a better person, and your life will turn around.

Q1.) What difficult path did you take? Was it worth the effort? Explain.

_____

_____

_____

_____

Q2.) Explain how self-control plays a part in your criminal thinking.

_____

_____

_____

_____

Q3.) Self-control is necessary to change my criminal thinking. True or False: Explain.

_____

_____

_____

_____

Q4.) While going down your difficult path, what setbacks did you encounter, and what would you have done differently to avoid the setbacks?

_____

_____

_____

_____

Q5.) Who did you hurt down your difficult path? And was it

worth the effort? Explain.

_____

_____

_____

_____

Q6.) Since you are a product of your decisions, what choices are you planning to change your criminal thinking after coming to the end of your difficult path?

_____

_____

_____

_____

Q7.) What kind of person do you want to become?

_____

_____

_____

_____

Group Activity

You will need a scarf, a timer, and a prize for this activity. The person administering the activity will bring a prize for the participants and a scarf full of knots. The participants will be asked one by one to try to untie each knot while saying a tongue twister and tie it back again in the same order. Instructions for the administrator are written in bold and should be read aloud to the participants.

Who's in for an activity to win a prize? It's a bit difficult task, but you have the chance to win something you'd like.

Wait for the participants to respond. Don't disclose the reward yet.

Let's start one by one; you are to untangle the many knots on this scarf, saying a tongue twister simultaneously. Once you have untied all knots, you will tie them back again.

The tongue twister goes like this:

"She sells the sea shells by the sea shore."

Time this activity for 1 minute each, and those who can do it within the designated time limit will be given a reward.

Just like this task, we have to go through difficult paths in life. Those paths don't necessarily have to be rewarding. A good life is a reward and worth struggle in the end. Just like untangling these knots can seem difficult but are rewarding toward the end, SO IS YOUR LIFE.

Chapter 3

Confront the Criminal in You

"If you get into crime, you got to know that everybody's a criminal and everybody's a liar, and everybody has the potential to backstab you because it's not an honest profession. So don't go into crime and look for honesty."

-Ice-T

Every person in this world is one bad day away from becoming a criminal. One wrong choice away from blurring the lines that differentiate right from wrong, moral from immoral. So, OUR CHOICES ARE IMPORTANT. Every day we are faced with different sorts of situations; some of these are bad, while others are not so much. How we react to these situations makes us law-abiding citizens, or we can become criminals.

As a recovering offender, you must be held accountable for your past, present, and future actions. Your criminal thinking and behavior are constantly being challenged. Therefore, you will have to learn to identify patterns in your thinking as direct means of understanding yourself.

Fact finder: By definition, the word "Criminal" is used as a term that allows someone to acknowledge and accept their criminality so that they may move into recovery.

Several people in our society believe there is no such thing as an ex-offender, only a recovering offender who must at all times be on alert of their thinking, which may allow them to avoid accountability and responsibility for their behavior. They also believe that you will be a convict for the rest of your life. Although you may not commit any more crimes, they believe that the minute your thinking returns unchecked to your former thought process, you will commit another crime.

Do you want to change the consequences of your behaviors?

If you are not concerned with the consequences, this workbook will not help you.

You have to confront the criminal in you and become fully aware of the thinking and behavior that has allowed you to escape accountability and responsibility for your behavior. This chapter will assist you in becoming aware of how your behavior has led to your incarceration and or parole/probation.

Since you are confronting the criminal in you, is it obvious that your thinking is different from a prosocial (positive, helpful behavior, promoting social acceptance and friendship) person? Which is the reason the crime that you committed makes sense to you. Will you agree that your criminal thinking aligns with an antisocial (a mental disorder in which a person consistently shows no regard for right and wrong and ignores the rights and feelings of others) person? You committed crimes because you were thinking rationally and justifying your behavior resulting from erroneous (flawed) thinking.

Your criminal thinking is allowing you to view yourself as a good person. It is why you truly believe or see yourself as a decent individual. Most criminals believe their actions are justifiable. Although you do not see how the same action is okay for another criminal, it is for you. It is already an accomplished fact when you think about what you want. For example, if you see someone you want to be in your life, it is already accomplished in your mind. You just need to complete the task.

As a criminal, you cannot entertain thoughts that would be harmless for prosocial people. If these thoughts begin to enter your mind, they must have something to alter or replace the thoughts with the right thoughts. The drug addict cannot even afford to begin to think about using. They are either on the road or have already relapsed if they do.

When confronting the criminal in you, every word, deed, and action that you say or do, which allows you to support your "uniqueness," has to be addressed to put the brakes on your thinking. Prosocial people are like criminals, and they also use criminal thinking errors. However, these thinking errors are not used in the same manner or to the same degree.

Fact Finder: Criminals lack empathy. That is, they cannot recognize and experience how others feel.

Several criminals believe that they may have to face their victim(s) in court. This crime becomes more personalized during this process, and in a criminal's mind, they believe that what they do is not personal. One of the most difficult assignments you can ask a criminal is to describe their victim(s)'s feelings while being victimized. It can be a very difficult task for any criminal. To complete this task, a criminal has to understand his thinking process before they can develop empathy for someone else.

One thing about criminals is that they either gain or lose power. They operate from extremes. When they are on top and have power, they're in a "God state." When they lose power, they are in "zero states." There is generally no middle ground. Also, another major focus of a criminal is the struggle for power and control. With power and control, the criminal always asks themselves the most popular question, "can I get away with it"?

There is a major difference between a criminal's criminal thinking process and that of a prosocial. To what degree are they willing to cover up the criminal acts of a fellow criminal? This is called the convict code, a (false) protection code supposed to allow a person to commit a crime without fear of being turned into authorities. The code is based on power, control, and fear. The code is enforced by people who refuse to accept responsibility for their behavior. The only one that these code benefits are the person who has the power. The code does not allow freedom and often breaks under the pressure of interrogation.

If you should express prosocial opinions regarding irresponsible behavior, you appear weak. The criminal feels like a person getting high when they commit a crime and does not get caught. The code works in this process by setting people up and controlling their behavior.

For example, the bubbles below suggest the thinking that criminals rationalize. The world should be suited as per their needs, as per their likings, and their beliefs. They have a high tendency to put themselves and their needs first.

When I don't have money, it's OK to break the law. (WRONG. Poverty isn't an excuse to commit crimes)

It's OK to use and manipulate others (WRONG, manipulation is one of the strongest examples of anti-social criminal thinking.)

The police are the reason for my problems. (WRONG, Your criminal behaviors is the reason for your problems. Your choices are yours and yours alone.)

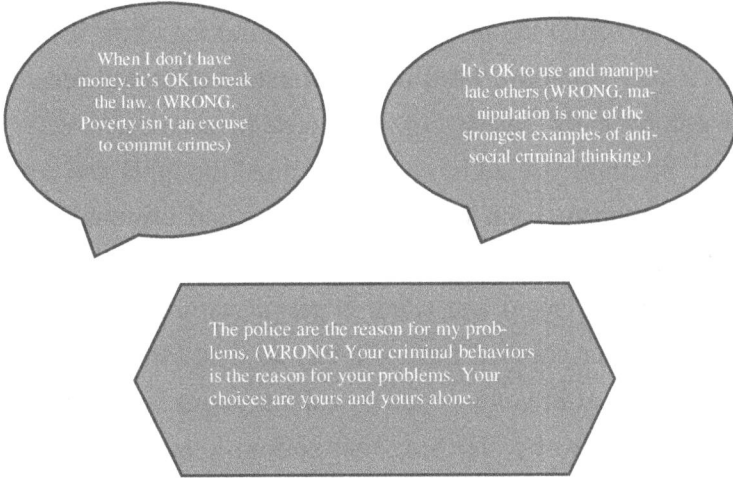

What aids criminal thinking in your mind? Criminals find themselves in constant denial that they are not true to themselves. Even though criminals are dishonest with themselves, they seldom notice or acknowledge their denial. Do you believe the only prison you need to keep yourself out of is the government-operated prison? Where will you be sent to after conviction? The reality is that you need to free yourself from the prison you are already in. The prison that is in your antisocial mind.

The only way you can free yourself from your internal prison is by confronting the criminal in you and starting the process of changing your criminal thinking. You must realize that you can change, and you have the potential to do it. However, the cycle goes this way.

- You are constantly defensive about your actions.
- You find yourself stuck in a situation where you don't listen and learn from your mistakes and actions.
- You will remain a prisoner within yourself. If your thinking doesn't change, your consequences will not change either.

Once you see that, you can't spend more time and effort remaining in denial about your criminal thinking. You'll become tired of this situation, tired of the negative consequences. You will not have the energy or resources to act defensively any longer. So, until you address your criminal thoughts and actions, you'll simply go back to your old ways and criminal thought processes.

If you feel caged and stuck in prison within your mind and you want to set yourself free, you can do this. First, by comforting the criminal in you, second by asking yourself if you want to change, and third by choosing that you no longer desire to play the criminal game. YOUR RECOVERY STARTS WITH YOUR WILL TO TRY. You can change yourself and turn your life around, but it starts with you.

"The hardest thing about changing your thought process is confronting the criminal in you."

So, to start confronting your criminal thinking, you need to start changing your current thought process to a much more responsible thought process. You also need to believe that your thought process will make good decisions that will positively affect your life. This will make you regain your trust and your self-esteem. In addition, it will give you the strength and faith to overcome most of your problems.

Q1.) Your criminal thinking and behavior are constantly being
_____?

Q2.) By definition, what is a "criminal"?

_____

_____

_____

_____

Q3.) What is a criminal considered to be for the rest of his or her life?

_____

_____

_____

_____

Q4.) What important question must you ask yourself prior to recovery?

_____

_____

_____

_____

Q5.) How does a criminal thinker allow them to view themselves?

_____

_____

_____

_____

Q6.) What is the difference between an antisocial person and a prosocial person using thinking errors?

_____

_____

_____

_____

Q7.) Why do you believe it is important for a criminal to have empathy for their victim(s)?

_____

_____

_____

_____

Q8.) To be in "God State," what does it mean?

_____

_____

_____

_____

Q9.) To be in "Zero State," what does it mean?

_____

_____

_____

_____

Q10.) What questions do Power and Control always carry with them?

_____

_____

_____

_____

Q11.) Do you find yourself suffering through self-inflicted consequences from your criminal thinking?

_____

_____

_____

_____

Q12.) Do you get defensive when people point out the negative
aspects of your personality, even if they are trying to help you?
____Yes ____No. Explain.

_____

_____

_____

_____

Q13.) While addressing your criminal thinking can trigger a lot
of things, only with self-reflections will you be able to get better.
Let's write down your triggers to know exactly what is affecting
your thinking, and then you can learn to change the negative outcome.

_____

_____

_____

_____

Q14.) Give an example of when you were in a "God State"?
How did it make you feel? Explain.

_____

_____

_____

_____

Q15.) What is the hardest thing about changing your thought process? Explain.

_____

_____

_____

_____

Group Activity

This group activity will require some acting and theatrics. (The administrator will ask people to volunteer for this next activity.) This chapter will enact a scene in which they will practically experience what they have learned about responsible thinking.

Person 1 is a police officer.

Person 2 is a criminal. (Bobby)

You are sitting in an interrogation room.

Police officer: So, you are back again, Big Bobby? What brings you here again?

Person 2: Robbery.

Police officer: Again? Bobby, we talked about this

Person 2: I didn't do it for myself this time.

Police officer: Then who did you do it for?

Person 2: (Bobby looking away) I needed to pay for some rent and some bills.

Police officer: So, you quit your job?

Person 2: I was fired.

Police officer: What do you want me to do now, Bobby? (disappointedly) Why were you fired?

Person 2: I didn't show up to work on time.

Police officer: For how long?

Person 2: For two days.

Police officer: And they fired you? Just like that? Come on. Tell me the truth.

Person 2: That is the truth.

Police officer: Really? Come on, man. We've been through this.

Person 2: Okay, fine! (In an annoyed tone)

Police officer: You were saying?

Person 2: I stopped showing up to work because they kept making me angry and started saying this like, don't do this. And don't do that. Wear this and not that.

Police officer: Bobby, that's literally what you have to do when you're working a job.

Person 2: I don't like being told what to do.

Scene End.

Now, let's discuss it.

Q1.) Do you agree with Bobby, or do you agree with the police officer? Explain.

_____

_____

_____

_____

Q2.) What's wrong with Bobby's attitude?

_____

_____

_____

_____

Q3.) What's wrong with Bobby's behavior?

_____

_____

_____

_____

Q4.) What should Bobby do to break free of the pattern he is stuck in?

_____

_____

_____

_____

Q5.) What changes does Bobby need to make to change his life?

_____

_____

_____

_____

Chapter 4

You're No Exception to the Rules

"No man is above the law and no man is below it; nor do we ask any man's permission when we require him to obey it. Obedience to the law is demanded as a right, not asked as a favor."

-Theodore Roosevelt

Do you wonder why you keep getting in trouble with the law?

Why do you make a lot of exceptions for yourself every time you get caught?

You blame your defiant and rule-breaking behavior on society. You must not forget that we live in a civilized society, and all communities follow the rules. Your circumstances are not special, and you do not get a pass every time you do something wrong.

Rules are alike for every person, and you are no exception. But your attitude toward the law is as if you need to follow these rules only when they suit you and go by your plans. If your thinking is wired in this way, it's not responsible thinking. It's going to lead you to criminal behavior and acts.

The habit of making exceptions for yourself is a bad one. Whenever you make exceptions for yourself, you develop a lack of self-discipline. You find yourself breaking the rules more often, and you can never recover from addiction or an unhealthy behavioral pattern if you make exceptions for yourself.

Resistance to the rules, resentment toward authority figures, and not following the law are all different sides of the same coin. It all boils down to the fact that you are not an exception. The world doesn't revolve around you, and you cannot make the world change for you, so you should change yourself. You should know that there's no use fighting here because these rules were made for your protection and the safety of others. So, you must follow them and not the other way around.

When you are indulging in criminal thinking, you are constantly engaging in dialogue with everyone around you. You are proving yourself to the world and are always defending your beliefs. So much so that you think about how these beliefs and attitudes are unhealthy and not suited for you. If you keep defending your criminal ideas and thinking, you will never develop responsible thinking.

If you dig deeper in your mind, you will find yourself not looking inward. Your focus on control, as psychology suggests, will be more outward. Criminal thinking is more self-serving, so you find yourself blaming the system, the rules, and the people when faced with problems. You find yourself complaining about everything. The thing about complaining is that it brings discouragement along. It takes away hope and responsibility, makes you less proactive, and prohibits responsible thinking.

If you have conditioned yourself to develop criminal thinking, you find yourself always convincing other people or constantly arguing how they are wrong and you are right. As a result, you are bothered, annoyed, agitated, and sometimes even angry when you notice that people are not paying any attention to what you are saying or doing; that is something according to you.

Consequently, you see the bad in people. According to Sigmund Freud, a popular psychologist and well-known as the father of psychology, people tend to protect their ego states by developing defense mechanisms when the reality is too troubling. A popular defense mechanism is a projection.

Criminally minded people project their behavior and thoughts onto other people. So, what they complain about in other people is actually about them. They project their negative traits onto others the same way as a projector or reflector would.

If you really ought to change yourself, you should know that you have got to learn not to act in hostility toward criticism. You have to take it for what it is feedback to improve you to be better. No matter what life throws at you, you have to learn to accept and understand it. It's not a perfect world, and we all have to face some problems or others. So, when you are faced with these circumstances, you should know that you are no exception to the rules, and you don't have to bend them. The world doesn't revolve around you, and it is you who has to change and not the world.

"It is only when you take responsibility for your life that you discover how truly powerful you are."

-Allamah Hunt

***

When you are on your life journey, and you think that you can no longer put up with becoming better and will fall into your old ways. Don't give in to it. You have to fight with every bone in your body, every tissue in every muscle, and it will take a lot of blood, sweat, and tears to recover finally. Recovery is a life-long process. It's not an adjective; it's a verb in a matter of speaking.

"The road to Recovery will not always be easy, but I will take it one day at a time, focusing on the moments I've dreamed about for so long."

-Amanda Lindhout

Let's talk about the hardest part of recovery.

Relapse.

What is relapse? It is to fall back into the former state of one's mind after a temporary improvement.

While you are on the road to recovery, you must think that

this is the end. A common mistake that people make while in recovery is to think that it is the destination when recovery is a journey in reality. As a result, they develop a cognitive distraction that is known as 'all-or-nothing' thinking.

According to them, you either recover fully, or you don't recover. However, it's not that simple in real life. While you are on your journey, you will be faced with many obstacles, roadblocks, or even hindrances, but you have to keep going, and you don't have to stop. Recovery ends when you stop picking up where you left the last time.

Therefore, take relapse as a temporary setback. Focus on the end goal: staying away from breaking the law, constantly making the right choices, and not manipulating people.

While you are on the journey of recovery, remember to believe in yourself. As cliché as it sounds, have faith in yourself. You've got this. You can for sure turn your life around, and you can make your life better. All you have to do is adopt responsible thinking every single day of the year, and undoubtedly you will change yourself. Hold yourself accountable for your mistakes, and discipline yourself.

Sticking to your current belief system is not only wrong according to the rules of civilized society. It's incredibly tasking mentally and physically. So, stop resisting other people and stop defending your erroneous belief system. It entails you to put an end to lying, arguing, and convincing other people of how you think the world should be.

The world doesn't revolve around one person. The law of the land was made for ALL, for the protection, order, and safety of us all.

If you act like a rebel or a deviant, you again excuse yourself from your situations and give yourself the advantage of making an exception. So, stop playing this game, stop blaming others and stop making exceptions for yourself. Discipline yourself like you would a toddler, but be stricter. Stop throwing a fit about the world and how the world should suit you.

Take the example of a person who wants to sell and smoke marijuana. You both hold the same approach toward life. A person who's been using believes that they want to quit and stop selling it, but the world is so tough for them and has always been. They give plenty of reasons why they think the world has been unfair and why they never stopped smoking or selling. To that person and you, the world seems like a maze. However, the regular person finds their way through this maze instead of complaining.

A criminal thinking person will find themselves complaining about the walls of the maze. Instead of becoming proactive and finding innovative solutions, they just sit there and complain. If you refuse to follow the rules and resist authority figures, you need to work on yourself. You need to change your attitude toward problems and setbacks.

A key component to developing a much more responsible thinking style is to become more adjustable. Psychologists worldwide attribute criminals and delinquents to being maladjusted individuals. Maladjustment is where it all begins. So, you must try and adjust to the society you are living in and make no exception for yourself. Once you follow the rules, you will find happiness and freedom and that your life is back on track. In addition, you will find yourself getting in less trouble with the law.

Q1.) Making exceptions for yourself is responsible thinking.
___True or ___False. Explain your answer:

_____

_____

_____

_____

Q2.) Authority Figures are the reason for your issues. Explain your answer:

_____

_____

_____

_____

Q3.) Why is recovery a lifelong process? Explain your answer:

_____

_____

_____

_____

Q4.) Because criminal thinking is a self-serving behavior, who do you find yourself blaming?

_____

_____

_____

_____

Q5.) Define Relapse.

_____

_____

_____

_____

Q6.) Explain why you have to accept that there are no rules except those that apply to your current situation.

_____

_____

_____

_____

Q7.) Based on what you have read in this chapter, explain, in your own words, how do you think your criminal thinking is no exception to the rules and how does it pertain to manipulating?

_____

_____

_____

_____

Q8.) Stress is part of daily life. We all find ourselves stressing about one thing or the other, whether it is our finances, health, families, or the outcomes of our actions. Now, sit and think about three things you stress about the most. After figuring it out, write it down and, in your own words, explain why the rules should not apply to you. Then challenge that with why they should apply

_____

_____

_____

_____

Q9.) Have you been in an argument with others? If so, what was it about? Could you have defused it, or are you still trying to be in control of things that you can't control?

_____

_____

_____

_____

Q10.) After completing this chapter, will you make a conscious effort to follow the rules at all times? ____Yes or ____No

Based on what you have read in this book? Write a paragraph about yourself.

Have you been following the rules of this book?

Yes: _____ No: _____

Group Activity

Case Study

Now let's all discuss a case of the law.

Jane is a social media influencer. The followers on her social media are hitting the number of millions. Her net worth is estimated at around $75 million. She is very famous and is adored by people and celebrities alike. One night she and her friends are partying.

One minute she finds herself taking shots the next minute, she finds herself in the car's driver's seat. She struggles to find her way home, and she can recall some of it, but it all looks very hazy to her. While she gains some perspective on the situation, she breaks the signal and hits a passenger at the zebra crossing. She's hit a man and his 6-year-old son, who are knocked out unconscious after hitting the bumper of her car. They both die instantly.

Now, do you agree or disagree with the following statements? Give reasons for your answers.

Q1.) She shouldn't have to go to jail because she's a celebrity.

_____

_____

_____

_____

Q2.) The judge shouldn't be as strict with her because she's America's sweetheart, and we should treat famous people differently.

_____

_____

_____

_____

Q3.) If the judge punishes her, it will lead to riots or even pro-
tests.

_____

_____

_____

_____

Q4.) It was an honest mistake, and she did try to stop the car, but
it was just bad timing that she couldn't.

_____

_____

_____

_____

Q5.) She should be treated like every other person and shouldn't
be given favor because of her celebrity status.

_____

_____

_____

_____

Q6.) Are there any exceptions to the rules or special circumstances, or should everyone be treated differently?

_____

_____

_____

_____

Chapter 5

The Face in the Mirror

"People who have had little self-reflection live life in a huge reality blind-spot."

-Bryant McGill.

When you look at yourself in the mirror, do you know who you are? Do you think about how things went wrong? Do you think about how and why you have ended up where you are in life? Sometimes, we are blinded by our true situation, and it's easy to look away from reality. But if you want to turn your lives around, you have to make yourself fully aware of yourself. This is where self-reflection comes in.

To simplify it, self-reflection means putting yourself under a microscope. Self-reflection entails that a person spends time and effort to evaluate, examine and look over their actions, thoughts, and beliefs. When a person takes out the time to reflect upon themselves, they make an effort to become aware of where they went wrong in life; it eventually leads them to find their own mistakes and flaws.

"Yesterday I was clever so I was changing the world. Today I am wise so I'm changing myself."

-Rumi

In the previous chapters, we have talked about how we have the psychological tendency to assume control over the situation as convicts. As criminals, we like the world to bend its rules when, in reality, we should be changing ourselves.

People with low self-esteem tend to make poor choices in life, so as a person actively struggling to make their lives better, you need to start reflecting on yourself. People with high self-esteem make better decisions as they hold themselves highly. An unhappy childhood, overly-critical parents, depression, high-risk teenage life is some causes of low self-esteem.

A research study conducted at the Indiana State University east linked high self-esteem to a reduced likelihood of crime. Results of the study suggested a negative association between self-esteem and criminal tendencies. In simpler terms, individuals having low self-esteem were more likely to commit a criminal act. On the other hand, individuals with high self-esteem were not as likely to opt for the criminal path.

Now, you can boost your self-esteem in several ways. First and foremost, you must adopt a more positive outlook toward life. You should practice gratitude and focus on what you already have. People with low self-esteem are overly critical of themselves and their environment, so make sure you lose the high-standard approach you have opted for throughout your life.

In the case of a person who is not on a criminal path, they set morals and establish role models earlier on in life. But the irony is that criminals who think highly of themselves and are self-absorbed are likelier to keep on the criminal path

A criminal person on the road to recovery must not hold a positive view of themselves because a criminal on the road to recovery will not be motivated to change their faulty beliefs or distorted thinking patterns. The mind of a criminal is distorted to the extent that a positive idea is a huge shift from reality. It will prevent a criminal from confronting reality.

For example, a criminal who has caused hurt to their friends and family is avoiding confrontation with reality if they are focusing on the positive things they have done for their family. Such a person is not on the path to recovery because this person is comfortable with reality which is a delusion.

When people do positive and good things while still committing criminal offenses, their good deeds further their destructive lifestyle. For example, a white-collar criminal who donates money to charity by evading taxes is not going to make an effort to change their current way of thinking because that person will be far too content with their current lifestyle.

Changing your thinking is not about doing good to reverse evil. It's accountability and taking responsibility for your negative actions. To recover, one must reflect upon their past and mistakes and take the necessary actions to improve their thinking and behavior.

Self-Reflection is a mental process you can use to grow your understanding of who you are, what your values are, and why you think, feel and act the way you do. When you self-reflect, you will become conscious of what drives you, and then you can make the necessary changes that will help you improve your life—also allowing you to recognize your strengths and limitations with a well-grounded sense of confidence and purpose.

Q1.) Define self-reflection.

_____

_____

_____

_____

Q2.) What worries you most about the future?

_____

_____

_____

_____

Q3.) What matters most in your life?

_____

_____

_____

_____

Q4.) When was the last time that you felt inspired?

_____

_____

_____

_____

Q5.) Are you taking time daily to do something selfish for yourself? Explain.

_____

_____

_____

_____

Q6.) In an ideal world, my one-year future-self will be _____.

What's something big or small that you want for your future self?

Once you have that answer, you can begin breaking it down and figuring out what small steps you can make in the next days/weeks/months to help you get there.

Group Activity

For this activity, we need two people, at least with an audience. It's a demonstrative role-play of what we've learned in the chapter. James and Bryan are roommates, and they are having a discussion. A moderator will moderate the session.

James: You stole my money, and now I am very upset.

Moderator: James feels frustrated.

Bryan: I know. But I also did the dishes for you and picked up the laundry. I've also made the bed.

Moderator: Bryan ignores the damage he is causing to James by his actions.

James: I have to pay the electricity bill. That money was designated for that. How will I pay the bill now?

Moderator: James is starting to feel resentful toward Bryan.

Bryan: I know. I thought maybe you should take the day off; I'll do the rest of the chores for you.

Moderator: James is resentful toward Bryan. Now, who is wrong in this scenario?

Answer: Bryan isn't taking responsibility for his actions.

Moderator: What is more likely to happen in the future?

Answer: Bryan will repeat his actions because he's too content to prove to James for stealing his money.

Moderator: How does this affect James?

Answer: James will grow resentful toward Bryan.

Chapter 6

Practicing Mindfulness

"How you think of yourself will have a tremendous impact on your future."

-Perrion Roberts

What is mindfulness? Mindfulness is the basic human ability to be fully present, aware of where we are and what we're doing, and not be overly reactive or overwhelmed by what's happening around us.

Stress and anxiety are a part of our everyday lives. As the times progress, we notice that the world is chasing excellence. Hence, every person is put under immense pressure. The pressure to excel more, achieve more and accomplish more all boils down to simply being ahead of the rat race. While stress is inevitable in this day and age, it's extremely important to learn how to deal with it. The outcome of stress is highly detrimental. It impacts the person's well-being, and I am not just talking about your psychological well-being and wellness. Stress affects your physical health, and it even weakens your immune system. Therefore, learning to cope with stress is pivotal to a person's recovery.

If you have just recently been incarcerated or released from jail, you might face a lot of stressors. Most of the time, these stressors can be found within you or might be present within your current situation. Whatever the case, maybe stress and worry about future circumstances are not always bad because they will motivate you to think ahead. However, suppose your stress is causing daily dysfunction and hindering your everyday tasks. In that case, you must learn adequate coping mechanisms to help deal with it or seek the help of mental health professional.

Dealing with stress can be very detailed, but it can become very easy and manageable once you get it. First and foremost, acknowledge that stress is an inevitable part of our lives. You cannot avoid it because it's unhealthy; the only to deal with stress is to learn to cope. Second of all, reflect upon yourself and identify the stressors in your environment. Then, jot them down and devise an individual strategy to deal with them.

A very modern and effective way to deal with stress is to learn to practice mindfulness. Today, it is being used by every person and has simply become a new way of life-a mantra to live by. Despite mindfulness being of Buddhist descent and an important clinical therapeutic technique in psychology, it is highly practical in our daily lives. It's being used in many prisons and correctional facilities across the country. Mindfulness refers to being present in daily situations and not elsewhere in our thoughts. It is defined as,

"...the basic human ability to be fully present, aware of where we are and what we're doing, and not overly reactive or overwhelmed by what's happening around us."

Now, you might wonder, are you not physically present? What does it mean to be fully present? I'll tell you what it means. You have to be focused and present in your situations and not be mentally absent elsewhere in your thoughts. When you are present in your family, you focus on them and not think about work. When you are out on probation or doing community service, you are actively aware of your doings and can look inward and be an active member.

When I thought of including this chapter in this book, it was clear. All the exercises and concepts we have studied, from deferred gratification to the chameleon game, end at mindfulness. Mindfulness stops you from criminal thinking; it is what enables you to think responsibly. It is mindfulness that helps you escape the prison within you. So even though this entire book is a great learning instrument and tool for those who wish to change, it would be to practice mindfulness if you were to take one thing away from it.

Mindfulness helps in your personal growth. It helps you get clarity, gain insight, be physically and mentally present, and helps you nurture the people around you by becoming a better version of yourself. All of your efforts are making to become a better person, and mindfulness-based behavioral practices are your knight and shining armor in this battle.

Whenever you are dealing with stress, remember the acronym COAL by Daniel J. Siegel, M.D. COAL stands for Curiosity, Openness, Acceptance, and last but certainly not least, Love. Dr. Siegel describes mindfulness as a mental state where you are curious to know the outcomes but don't let judgment get in the way. Have an open mind and heart to be aware of your circumstances and accept them wholeheartedly instead of making excuses or exceptions. Lastly, and it may sound cliché, love yourself despite your choices and the situation you find yourself in.

This acronym can help you become more mindful when dealing with situations that trouble you. It is a dummy formula for responsible thinking. By going through this pattern of COAL -Ing, you'll know what to do when making amends and out in real life away from the correctional facility. And when you are out and can't figure out what to do, just remember to COAL your way to situations.

Practicing mindfulness in your daily life is very important. Mindfulness-based practices include body-positive exercises such as yoga, workout, walking, or physical activity. Being physically active can be a very practical way to practice mindfulness and can help you become more mindful of your body. In addition, practicing gratitude and focusing on what you have, whether in journaling or taking 5 minutes out of your time every day just to practice and recall your blessings, will help you focus on the positive things in life.

Senses are an important part of practicing mindfulness. Make sure you use your senses when you are practicing mindfulness. I will be attaching an extremely helpful mindfulness technique at the end of this chapter. It's called the *'Five Senses Mindfulness Exercise.'* It can help you become more present in your situations.

As mindfulness has its root in Buddhist culture, meditation and yoga can help calm your nerves down and focus on the present. It is an incredibly helpful mindfulness technique. Focus your energy on your actions and your body while performing yoga. Remember, just as yoga calms down the tensions in your back muscles, meditation and mindfulness relax the stresses in your mind. You can find plenty of videos on YouTube that can help you do mindfulness yoga at home!

Breathing is an often neglected but important part of healing. Our breathing reflects our state of behavior; we often find ourselves out of breath when we are stressed. So, whenever you're experiencing anxiety, start deep breathing. It will help calm you down and relieve your stress. Many deep breathing exercise videos on the internet can help you practice mindful breathing.

Check-in with yourself more often than usual. How are you doing emotionally? Are you feeling overwhelmed? What exactly are you feeling? Identification of your feelings is an important part of emotional regulation. The wheel below can help you identify what you feel if you cannot word them.

You can Let it RAIN if you are overwhelmed by something,

you can *'Let it RAIN!'* To let it RAIN means **R**ecognizing what's going on (self-awareness), **A**llowing yourself to experience it. **I**nvestigate it using your observations and thoughts, and **Non-identify** with it by detaching it from yourself as a situational circumstance and not a depiction of who you are.

Often, mindfulness is associated with being calmer and relaxed. While this is true in most cases, many people struggle with practicing mindfulness techniques, especially when they

are energetic people. Practicing mindfulness can help you hold your energy levels by regulating them. So, when you find yourself getting bored and your energy level spikes, try exercising, running, or sprinting. You can even do yoga which can help you regulate your energy levels.

A lot of people struggle with having to deal with fears. These fears can be as small and insignificant as a small insect or can be so enormous that it hinders the person struggling with them. In extreme cases, it can even turn into a phobia.

Modern research suggests that while many expensive psychotherapies are designed and catered to treating phobias and fears, practicing mindfulness-based therapy can be useful in altering a more effective approach to unlearning those responses. While practicing mindfulness, people re-process old and previously threat-inducing memories or thoughts by making meaningful and less-threatening connections in their brains.

A lot of people struggle with experiencing feelings of worthlessness. Feeling worthless and uninspired is a terrible feeling, and it can get the best of us. Feeling worthless is associated with childhood trauma, having experienced failure, setbacks, and negative feedback. By practicing mindfulness, you can nurture your self-esteem and improve your self-image.

On the opposite side of the spectrum, if you have an inflated sense of ego, it can give rise to unhealthy pride. People who have unhealthy pride can get control of their situation because mindfulness preaches moderation.

Among the many things practicing mindfulness can help a person, the most note-worthy mention is anger control. Anger is a healthy emotion, especially if it's experienced in response to being treated unfairly or receiving unjust treatment. However, unnecessary spikes of anger can be bad for a person's mental and physical health. Engaging in practices such as deep breathing and being present at the moment can help you get to the bottom of your anger, hence fixing the situation that gave birth to feelings of anger.

Mindfulness is a lifestyle. You are on to this new and improved lifestyle, so you must focus on yourself and become this person who is a responsible citizen and a great human being. I know this chapter may come off as overly ambitious, but you can take away many things from it. Most of these techniques and practices are centered on modifying your outlook toward life.

Becoming mindful will impact your entire life. It will affect how you eat, sleep, breathe, and function as a person. If you start focusing your energy on becoming a grounded individual, everything we have learned in this book will follow suit.

Q1.) Do you find yourself struggling with stress and anxiety? If so, then when?

_____

_____

_____

_____

Q2.) Write down the thoughts you have when you are feeling anxious.

_____

_____

_____

_____

Q3.) How do you cope with stress? Practice mindfulness as a solution.

_____

_____

_____

_____

Q4.) Do you find yourself struggling with sudden outbursts of anger?

_____

_____

_____

_____

Q5.) What do you do to deal with your anger? Do you practice mindfulness to calm yourself down? Explain.

_____

_____

_____

_____

Q6.) What are the things that make you angry?

_____

_____

_____

_____

Q7.) Do you sometimes feel worthless? Write down what you feel. Add mindfulness as your solution.

_____

_____

_____

_____

Q8.) What are some of your achievements in life? Write 5 achievements. They can be both big and small.

_____

_____

_____

_____

10 Minute Mindfulness Worksheet

Take the time to reflect on some of your life's positive moments. For this exercise, wear an imaginary spectacle of positivity. Then, you'll look back on the brightest highlights of your life.

Task 1 - Write the names of three of the most important people in your life to who you feel most close.

1. _____
2. _____
3. _____

Task 2 – Recall the names of three places in the world that you value the most and have good memories associated with.

1. _____
2. _____
3. _____

Task 3 – What are three things that you own that you love and adore the most? Be specific in writing those things down that have helped you positively in the past.

1. _____
2. _____
3. _____

Task 4 – Write your top three treasured accomplishments over the past few decades.

1. _____

2. _____

3. _____

Task 5 – Write three things you are passionate about and wish to pursue shortly.

1. _____

2. _____

3. _____

Task 6 – What are three things you are most looking forward to in the present?

1. _____

2. _____

3. _____

Task 7 - Can you name at least one thing in life that you believe is going great? It can be anything.

_____

_____

_____

_____

Group Activity

"Shared Compassion"

For this activity, each group member has to write down a few things we will discuss in the group.

First Task – Write a memory from your past that is painful for you to recall.

_____

_____

_____

_____

_____

_____

_____

_____

_____

_____

_____

Second Task – Now that everyone has written what memory pains them the most, each person will discuss the memory in the group one by one. And each time a member shares a painful memory, group members will respond with an empathetic remark.

The Five Senses Worksheet

Earlier, we talked about how engaging in a sensory experience is present in the moment. You can write it down for now, but this can be done in your mind by making a mental note.

Sense of Sight - Write five things you can see.

1. _____
2. _____
3. _____
4. _____
5. _____

Sense of Touch - Write five things you can touch.

1. _____
2. _____
3. _____
4. _____
5. _____

Sense of Hear - Notice five things you can hear

1. _____
2. _____
3. _____
4. _____
5. _____

Sense of smell - Write five smells you can observe.

1. _____
2. _____
3. _____
4. _____
5. _____

Sense of taste - Write one thing you can taste

1. _____
2. _____
3. _____
4. _____
5. _____

Chapter 7

Let Go of the Chameleon Game

"Nurture your own confidence and make it real; don't pretend to be someone you're not."

-Tom Hiddleston

A personality trait that can cause trouble is pretending to appear like someone you are not. This personality trait is often referred to as hypocrisy. Hypocrisy is bad as it entails being honest and true to who you are as a person. Aspiring to become someone or holding an image you wish to keep is not the same as pretending to appear like someone else.

Showing that you are a different person is an act that can get frustrating for you as time passes by. You will have to put in extra effort to show people this objectified persona of yourself, and often, people will find out who you truly are. However, it's also incredibly taxing mentally and emotionally and can drain you out.

If you have appeared to be different from different people in various situations and circumstances, you also have a habit of not being true to yourself. Even though it may start as real inspiration, things can quickly turn sour in the beginning. You may find yourselves pretending to be someone else, so much so that you lose track of who you are as a person. Consequently, you lose yourself in the process.

Have you ever seen chameleons? A chameleon is a reptile that is quite famous for changing its color. Its color-changing feature is known as 'camouflaging.' Even though many wild animals tend to camouflage when they sense danger from predators, chameleons are particularly famous for it.

A noteworthy mention is religiosity. The term religiosity refers to believing in a divine power greater than one's own. It also describes the concept of spirituality. Modern research supports the idea that having a belief system promotes emotional and spiritual well-being. Attending Mass on Sunday or being part of your local religious community can help you become a well-adjusted person.

Religiosity is unique in its own way, as religions throughout the globe teach their followers to become a better version of themselves. It teaches a person to abide by the law, not to become a hypocrite, and contribute to society in the best way they seem fit. If you struggle to find your own unique identity, reconnecting with God or whatever spiritual power you believe in will help.

A study done by Oxford University on the relationship between religiosity and self-esteem in later life revealed that old adults tend to have higher self-esteem and have a strong morality, implying that religiosity, self-esteem, and self-image have a positive correlation.

The Chameleon Case Study

Let's take the case study of a chameleon to understand closely what we're talking about. The defining characteristic of a social chameleon is similar to how a chameleon in wildlife can change colors rapidly. They can adjust to social situations. They can blend in with any kind of circumstance that they are put into.

Social chameleons are quiet and reserved people. They don't act out of the ordinary or act like they are the life of the party. As a result, they find themselves blending in social situations. For example, if they plan to become a drug dealer, they will imitate that community's person behind the business, i.e., the King or Queen Pin. Hence, they'll alter their mind to criminal thinking and behavior.

Social flexibility is a very useful skill, which can be very useful for any person. However, that is not a good thing in the case of criminal thinking. It's in the person's psyche to feel included in social situations. Socially flexible people can mold, adjust, and re-invent themselves according to life's challenges. These people then become professional liars. They adapt to the changes in life and take advantage of situations.

The reality of life is that any person can be subjected to becoming a social chameleon. Sometimes it starts as admiration and, little by little, takes over your life as you are so habitual of doing these things that you start doing them unconsciously.

For example, do you mimic a person's talking style from a different country? Do you find that your accent suddenly is now eccentric?

Q1.) Do you believe that your behavior in the past has been similar to that of a chameleon? Explain.

_____

_____

_____

_____

Q2.) Do you think you easily start copying other people's ways of talking and speaking after spending time with them? Explain?

_____

_____

_____

_____

Q3.) Are you a chameleon?

_____

_____

_____

_____

Q4.) A chameleon is a reptile that can change its color to blend in with its surroundings. Has your past behavior been similar to the actions of a chameleon?

_____

_____

_____

_____

Q5.) Describe one situation in which you attempted to fool someone into believing you were a different type of person than you already are.

_____

_____

_____

_____

Q6.) What are the dangers of having a chameleon personality?

_____

_____

_____

_____

Q7.) What was the outcome of your efforts?

_____

_____

_____

_____

Q8.) What have you done to change your chameleon-like personality?

_____

_____

_____

_____

Chapter 8

Living Your Life On Life Own's Terms

"The moment you accept responsibility for EVERYTHING in your life, is the moment you gain the power to change ANY-THING in your life."

-Hal Elrod

Living life on your own terms means having purpose and fulfillment in your life and having freedom and flexibility to do what matters most to you. It's important to do this because how you feel about your life affects you and everyone around you.

Many people go through life without a purpose or plan, which sets the stage for their criminal thinking. You will start to feel stuck in your mind, believing that the only way to provide for your family is to commit crimes.

A lot of times, people make the grave mistake of thinking that their life is supposed to be perfect. They believe that people around them have been blessed with a good life. They think that life is fair for everyone around them but them. Now, reflect on your past and consider whether or not you know someone who perhaps has struggled more than you have. Now, you must acknowledge that people around you, your friends, family, and relatives, have dealt with more. Take inspiration from them. If they can do it, so can you!

When these situations make their way to your life, always remember that you are not alone. Your circumstances are not special. People around you have been in the worst scenario in the past and have faced those challenges head-on. So, change your thinking little by little. You can start by focusing on things that are actually in your control. Sometimes, tough times bring out the personality traits that even you were not aware of. Once you deal with the setbacks of your life, you will notice that your self-respect will escalate, and your sense of self-worth will increase.

The best way to overcome life's challenges is first by accepting that things will not always be perfect, and hence you should prepare for the bad times in advance. Life is not smooth, and as the saying goes, a smooth sea never made a skillful sailor. So, don't fall behind in the face of adversity because someone once said that adversity often masks itself underneath opportunity. So, prepare yourself for negative outcomes that you may think will come.

Having a backup plan or a contingency plan is very important. In case of a relapse or an accident, your backup plan will keep you moving toward the destination of your choice. In life, hope for the best because hope is important. It is something we look forward to. But always anticipate and prepare for the worst beforehand, so you never have to act irresponsibly in these situations.

Here are 6 simple tips to help you change your criminal thinking and start living life on your terms.

Dream

It starts with knowing how you want your life to look and who you want to share this dream with. What are some of the dreams and goals you have always wanted since you were a child? What did you always dream about being when you grew up?

Consider Where You Are Right Now

After you dream a little, next, you want to consider your current situation your reality. What are you doing currently? Is what you are doing moving you closer to those dreams and goals? Or are you stuck in a situation that is out of your control? Take a few minutes to assess your life and current situation.

Think about the Past

Next, did your criminal thinking bring you closer to your dreams and goals in the past, or did it just push it completely out of your reach? What have you tried in the past to bring your dreams to life? Maybe you attempted to launch a drug business.

Was this your dream as a child? Consider your past thinking, has it helped you get any closer to your ideal life?

Assess Your Options

Now, assess your options. What can you change in your current situation that will help you get closer to living life on your own terms? Do you need to consider a career change? Restructure your thinking and focus on your goals for the future.

Start thinking of a list of potential options. Don't count yourself out or assume you can't do something – just write down everything that comes to your mind.

Talk to someone else who is living life on their own terms. It is helpful to get the perspective of someone who is already where you want to be. This is why it's important to start with what you want your life to look like. It will be easier to identify others who are living the way you want to be if it's clear in your own mind.

Make a Plan

Once you are done brainstorming, and you've talked to others who are living life on their own terms, you're ready to make a plan. Considering your current situation, it's unlikely that you can create the life you want. You will need to make a plan. Start after your release date, depending on how far away that date is set. **But if you don't write it down and create a plan, it's not going to happen!**

Once you've created an overall plan to live life on your own terms, break it down into 90-day goals and objectives. This makes it less overwhelming and easier to accomplish.

Team up and Take Action

Finally, take action! If you don't start, you'll always have criminal thinking and never create the life you long for. In order to change criminal thinking, you have to start taking steps toward your goals each and every day, regardless of your current situation, to make it happen. It helps to have an accountability partner or a team to support you along the way. When you team up with others working toward living life on their own terms, you'll be much more likely to stay motivated and find success.

Q1.) Describe three situations where you felt that life has been unfair to you?

_____

_____

_____

_____

Q2.) Describe what your thoughts were while you were in those situations. What actions did you take, or could you have taken to make the situation better?

_____

_____

_____

_____

Q3.) What can you do now to turn this negative situation into an opportunity or personal strength?

_____

_____

_____

_____

Q4.) What is your backup plan for life and finances in case things start to go south for you?

_____

_____

_____

_____

Group Activity

We will keep this group activity simple. Here are a few lines that, if repeated daily, can foster a healthy change in you. In this session, we will be repeating and discussing these lines multiple times.

"Life will not always go my way. I will hit unexpected road bumps. There are problems that are bound to happen, and I shall persevere through them. Things will get better. The times will change, and I will be happy again."

Now each person in the group must discuss a situation where they felt that their life had no purpose and how are they planning to live life on their own terms.

Chapter 9

The Hardest Prison to Escape is In Your Mind

"As I walk out the door toward the gate that will lead to my freedom, I knew if I didn't leave my bitterness and hatred behind, I'd still be in prison."

-Nelson Mandela

We discussed why it is important to confront the criminal within you in the previous chapter. We also practiced how and when you can do this. Finally, we talked about how people who have criminal-like thinking are stuck in an internal prison of their own making.

If you are reading this book, you should acknowledge that you engaged in self-destructive behaviors at some point in your childhood or adolescence. These behaviors follow you through your journey in life. Somewhere along that time, you developed a habit of blaming other people. If you found it harder to concentrate in school, you simply blamed your teachers or your course for being too difficult. You were stuck in a cycle where you were criticized by your parents, siblings, and teachers. You were constantly told that you would end up in jail or dead. At this point, you started believing and acting like this.

You were a careless teenager who needed some hope and belief growing up. So, you must acknowledge that you, too, were a victim of physical and mental abuse at some point in life.

If you keep nurturing this attitude of believing that there is no point in trying anymore, you will end up hurting yourself even more. You will also find yourself not reaching your full potential, and your spiritual and mental growth as a person will be stunted.

This cycle of criticism from family and elders that we discussed earlier is vicious. Your deviant behavior and practices caused you to go and become more self-destructive. The more you were doubted, the more you doubted yourself.

The more self-doubt you engage in, the lower your self-esteem, so you start feeling inferior and more distant from people. When you start withdrawing yourself from friends and family, you become unsure of yourself. You think you lack control over your own life.

You have to start motivating yourself. Self-motivation is the key to setting yourself free from the internal prison you are in. You have to reclaim your life. With the appropriate amount of motivation within yourself, you can fulfill your dreams and ideas. If you dreamed of achieving a certain lifestyle and now it seems impossible, always know that good things happen to people who believe in themselves. If you motivate yourself, you can open the locked door to opportunities.

If you feel that you were restricted or limited at some point in your life, you will get to know that this affects your experiences, your ability to grow, and your exposure to the environment. If you are restricted, you will find that you will not achieve greater things in life. You should know that life is limitless, and success knows no boundaries. If you want to achieve glory, even the sky is not the limit. So, don't restrict yourself. Instead, improve and work on yourself.

In Social Psychology, a very well-known term explains people's reactions to situations as bystanders or spectators. It's called the bystander effect. The bystander effect mentions that people have a responsibility to react to circumstances. For example, a person with criminal thinking fails to take responsibility into their own hands.

If you have a bystander's attitude, you will find yourself not being able to help a person who needs help. You will find yourself waiting for other people to come and help and fail to do it yourself. You need to know that we all have a responsibility in these situations. So, you must actively participate in making such situations better.

You need to know that if you are unhappy with your lifestyle, you need to change it. You can make your life become better. A better life starts with your will to try. And when you have started trying, don't waste yourself by putting in all the effort at once. Instead, take small, consistent baby steps, and you will find yourself quickly climbing the ladder of success.

So, picture it this way. Your life is like a house that has caught fire. Right now, your responsibility is to stop the fire physically if you can or call someone to help you stop it. This book will help you stop the fire that is in your house. Instead of acting like a bystander, get up and change how you think and then change your life.

This chapter is about breaking the prison that you are inside. You are immensely talented, and you have a lot of potential. However, if you feel self-restricted or imprisoned, you are not reaching your maximum potential. Self-restriction acts like blockages that limit your growth. They act as obstacles to your personal growth and development. Once you break free of the shackles of your mind, you will discover your talents, and you will use them to your advantage and change your criminal thinking and live a more responsible and mentally free life

Q1.) What self-destructive behaviors did you engage in at some point in your childhood? _____Yes ____No. Explain.

_____

_____

_____

_____

Q2.) In what ways can you adapt to open the locked door? Write them down.

_____

_____

_____

_____

Q3.) Do you sometimes find yourself being imprisoned even though you are not behind bars? If you do so, please elaborate on how.

_____

_____

_____

_____

Q4.) What situation in your life caused you to become a by-stander or spectator to it? Write it down.

_____

_____

_____

_____

Q5.) What change do you think you can make to change your

bystander attitude toward the problems in your life?

_____

_____

_____

_____

Group Activity

For this activity, the entire group has to be divided into two sub-groups, A and B. The participants of group A will think of negative experiences, and the participants of group B will find positive ways to interpret the situation in 40 seconds. Make a score-card. If group B cannot respond or lacks to find positives, they get a 0, and Group A gets a 1.

Score Sheet

Group A		Group B

Chapter 10

Become Adaptable to Circumstances

"A wise man adapts himself to circumstances, as water shapes itself to the vessel that contains it."

-Chinese Proverb

Your current circumstances force you to change your criminal thinking and evaluate and reinvent perspectives in life and the choices you've made.

Once you are incarcerated, the jail or prison forces you to become adaptable to your current circumstances. Your ability to adapt to jail or prison and be able to become comfortable with the ever-changing circumstances in your life will influence your happiness, health, stress, and well-being.

Since being incarcerated is your current situation, we know that you are uncomfortable and have severe panic attacks, but remember that it is all because of your criminal thinking and actions. Jails and prisons are designed to be uncomfortable from the lack of privacy, standards of beds, and the quality of foods you eat. However, because of the changes in your life, you must embrace the ability to adapt to your circumstances. It will allow you to reduce stress and anxiety around these new changes.

Adaptability is your ability to move in a given direction at any time. In previous chapters, we have discussed how selfishness and thinking that others should change themselves for you is a distorted characteristic of criminal thinking. To reform criminal thinking, you must know and acknowledge that your situations are not new, and the world certainly doesn't revolve around you. Criminal thinking and a person's mental state of mind often put them in situations where they are compromised of life's beautiful things.

So, when life gets tough, learn to roll with the punches. Rather than changing your surroundings or the people around you, learn to adapt to your current circumstances. Because at the end of the day, you can truly only change yourself and not others. Every person in this world is going through something or the other. Trials and tribulations are a part of life.

In the midst of the Covid-19 pandemic, many people have suffered from unemployment, financial and health-related crises, and the loss of their loved ones. When you connect your problems to the world and acknowledge that everyone is going through something or the other, you realize that you are not alone. You are the smallest part of a big universe that has to learn to adapt to your current circumstances.

In this world today, a person has to be willing to learn, make mistakes, change their criminal thinking and learn some more. When entering into your current circumstances, you can adjust your criminal thinking to produce positive and productive results.

Most of the time, when a person is put into a new situation, there are a lot of expectations going on in their minds. Some of which come from past personal experiences, mistaken beliefs, or other people's experiences. We then form our own conclusion about what will happen based on our own beliefs, and those beliefs typically will affect our choices or actions.

In every situation we are involved in, we go through it with expectations, requirements, and desires.

•**Expectation:** A strong belief that something will happen.

•**Requirements:** What we need or want to happen.

•**Desires:** A strong feeling of wanting something to happen.

The power to adapt to your current circumstances lies in understanding what these expectations, requirements, and desires actually are. It's about closing the gap between the risks that we see in the changes within our current situations.

Also, we like to seize all opportunities from those risks.

In jail or prison, circumstances are always evolving and changing. Your ability to adapt can increase your chances of being released early. Every day of our lives, we are always experiencing unpleasant and uncomfortable things. Some of those things are within our control, but being incarcerated, they are not.

Adaptability ensures that you stay focused on things that are bringing you down. This will allow you to bounce back from inevitable failures. To become more adaptable in your life while incarcerated, you must learn the ability to take action without knowing the outcome and act without any expectations will be your driving force to change your criminal thinking and embrace the changes.

Today is the day that you must learn the power of adaptability so that you are ready, willing, and able to take on any changes in your current situation that will come your way.

> *"It is not the strongest or the most intelligent who will survive but those who can best manage change."*
> *–Charles Darwin*

Q1.) What is Adaptability?

_____
_____
_____
_____

Q2.) Why is adaptability so important while incarcerated?

_____
_____
_____
_____

Q3.) How do you demonstrate adaptability?

_____
_____
_____
_____

Q4.) What five things can you do to become adaptable to your circumstances?

_____
_____
_____
_____

Group Activity

For this group activity, bring objects and scatter them on the floor. Recruit at least 4 participants for two sets of each. Now one partner is supposed to pick up the scattered stuff while being blindfolded, and the second one will guide them from afar.

Whoever finds the stuff fastest wins the game. This game can be done with more than 4 people.

Just like you are blindfolded and cannot see, and the other person can see but cannot reach for it, life will throw curveballs at you, and you have to adapt and improvise to your life circumstances.

Chapter 11

Prepare Yourself for Lots of Downtimes and Life Changes

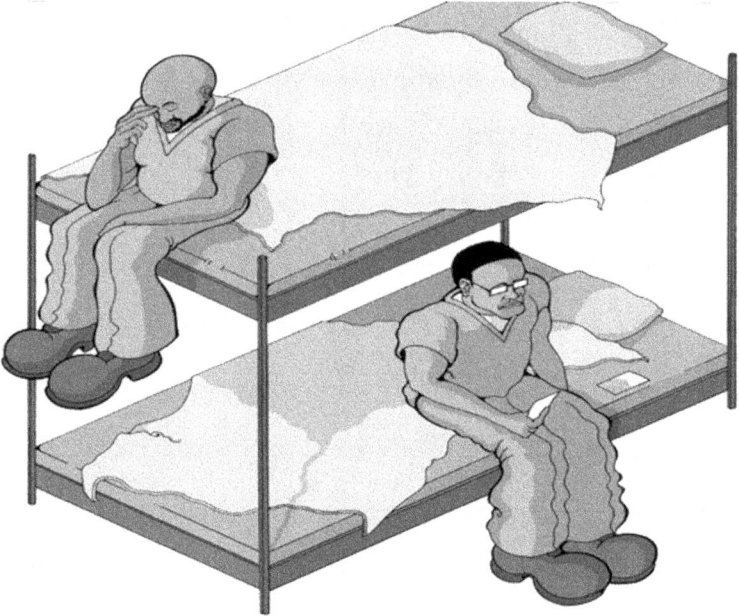

"Life is not always perfect. Like a road, it has many bends, ups, and downs, but that's its beauty."

-Amit Ray, World Peace

In the previous chapter, we discussed how life is not perfect. However, it is essential to prepare in advance if you have been convicted of a criminal offense. No matter the nature of your offense, your confinement will disrupt your normal life.

Once you know that you will be going to prison, the first thing you must do is prepare your family. Because they will be devastated by the idea of you being locked up, it may take them a while to come to terms. First, however, you have to sit down and talk with them, especially in preparing your children. If you have young children, they may not understand the long-term implications of your absence, but it will soon affect them. So you need to make a plan that will help them to cope with your absence. You should really consider consulting a psychologist. In fact, they will be able to help you and your children to cope with this disruption.

You also need to organize your finances, which will include appointing a Power of Attorney this way, you can create a budget for the care of your children and how the money will be channeled to your commissary account. Before you surrender to prison, you must identify a primary point of contact. Also, you need to make a Doctor's and Dental appointment. Although the service is available in prison, it may not match the standards of your current providers.

Adequate prison preparation will ease the transition to your new life behind bars. It might not take away the hard realities that follow losing your freedom, but knowing what to expect and how to navigate your life inside the jail or prison can be the difference between a smooth transition and a turbulent outset. It is so hard losing your freedom, especially when it comes to your emotional and psychological well-being.

A long period of incarceration equals a lot of available downtime on your hands, which can be positive or negative; it is totally up to you. Life is sometimes just boring and not as exciting every single day. The reality of life is that there is not always going to be an adventure on board, and you will spend a large chunk of your time doing routine tasks that will not be very interesting.

Generally, criminal conviction comes with potentially life-changing consequences, and the period before incarceration will be the hardest for you and your family. Once you are incarcerated, your life changes, such as; your time will be spent on chores rather than watching people on social media platforms or performing skits on Tik Tok. Yet, these boring basic things are what will steer the boat of your life in a positive direction.

It's not always being locked up or being incarcerated that can bring you down in life. If you are not making the most out of your circumstances, you are in prison whether or not you are behind bars. If you are not making lemonades from the lemons that life throws at you, you need to start changing yourself. Spend your time making good decisions, taking a much more positive route, whether mentally or physically imprisoned.

If you are about to be given parole or are on parole right now, know that you have all this time on your hands to work on yourself. Engage in three things.

1. Reflection on your past,

2. The acknowledgment of your current situation accepting the consequences and circumstances.

3. Modifying your behavior for the future. (Change your thinking) You must change your past behavior in order not to repeat past mistakes. Use this time to identify unhealthy behav-

ior patterns, faulty thought processes, and beliefs in the following way

Criminal Behavior		_Responsible Behavior_
Criminal behavior often starts with boredom, the desire or attempt to get a "charge" or "rush" out of life.	_VS._	_Responsible behavior life's details must focus on completing all tasks on a regular basis._

Changing criminal thinking is a process, but it is up to you to work toward the crime-free life you desire. Changing criminal behavior starts with making positive, responsible choices, which leads you to have responsible behavior. Responsible behavior can sometimes lead to boredom. You must keep in mind that the possibility of relapse is always present. It's up to you to stay on the road to recovery. You are fighting for your life, a prison-free life. Remember, you must never get tired of doing the right thing.

Here are a few helpful examples of things to try when you feel bored. Attending church functions and self-help groups like NA and AA and engaging in positive conversations with others who can relate to your struggles—focusing on the next positive choices for yourself. Exercising, drawing, and meditation are also helpful. It is good to have the phone numbers and locations of these resources nearby. They will be good tools to have when faced with the boredom of downtime.

Q1.) Describe three routine tasks that you complete successfully and regularly.

1._____

2._____

3._____

Q2.) What are five positive activities you can plan to do when you feel bored?

1._____

2._____

3._____

4._____

5._____

Q3.) What are you doing to prepare yourself for lots of down-time and life changes?

_____

_____

_____

_____

_____

_____

_____

Group Activity

For this exercise, divide the participants into 3 groups at least. Then, present a threatening situation through which they have to survive through.

They are stuck on an expedition to the arctic pole, and their leader has gotten frostbite on his hands and feet, making him unable to move. The cold wind has caused the team to develop snow blindness, and their vision is impaired. They have to listen to the advice of their team leader and make a shelter by using sticks, a large cloth, and cardboard paper. This activity will teach them the importance of socialization in times of crisis and survival techniques.

Chapter 12

Life Assessment

"It's never too late to become who you want to be. I hope you live a life that you're proud of, and if you find that you're not, I hope you have the strength to start over."

-F. Scott Fitzgerald

Don't blame other people if you find yourself unable to tackle a situation or life's circumstances. Stand up and accept responsibility. Don't shift the liability on others. Take responsibility for your own actions. Take some time out and look back to a point in your life when you decided that led you to where you are right now. It's an absolute waste of time to blame other people, and it can get you nowhere in life. In order to achieve greatness, it's important for you to realize where you are at fault and fix it.

If you have recently gotten out of prison, adjusting to the new beginnings in life can be tough. However, you should never forget that it's the exact opportunity that you are looking for to start fresh and have a new beginning. The world can seem overwhelming at first, but you can succeed if you want to. You just need to learn the right skills, such as social skills and problem-focused coping techniques. These kinds of skills will help you find your way in life.

If you prepare yourself, you have the opportunity to become successful in your life after prison.

"Rather than viewing a brief relapse back to inactivity as a failure, treat it as a challenge and try to get back on track as soon as possible."
-Jimmy Connor

We have discussed how important it is to modify your thinking from criminal thinking to responsible thinking in the previous chapters. As the book progresses, we have gone through many different strategies to help change our behavior. Now, considering that you are actively working on yourself and applying all that you have studied yourself, you might have come across a few instances where you have reverted to your old ways. Unfortunately, this means that you have relapsed.

Let's talk about what happens when a person relapses. You were working on yourself, watching every move you make, modifying each step you are taking, and thinking things through. And then, all of a sudden, things go foul. With one wrong choice, you make you find yourselves in the same dirt and rubble as before. Now, you are experiencing all sorts of feelings. You feel like a failure; you feel like a loser or, at the very least – a lost cause.

You would find yourself experiencing guilt and shame. And you ask yourself.

What really is the point of all this?

What is the point of trying when you can't change yourself?

If you are having these thoughts, then park them. Don't move ahead. Let's talk about these thoughts. This kind of thinking pattern is called 'all-or-nothing' thinking. What you do in all-or-nothing thinking is that you interpret the situation as a whole outcome. However, that is usually not the case.

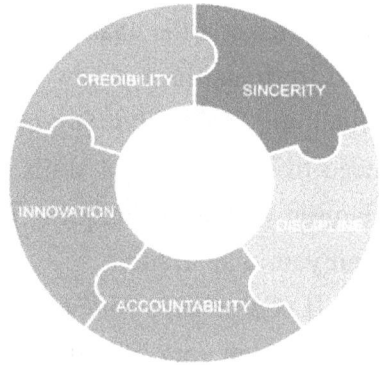

Just because you have had a setback or a relapse doesn't mean that it's too late and it's all over. After a relapse, the emotions you experience, coupled with guilt and shame, make you feel that it is the end of the world. What you need to remember is that setbacks are bound to happen.

When you are trying to achieve something, anything that may be, you'll find yourself failing before truly getting the hang of it. So, if you have had a relapse, you should know that it will happen, and it's going to happen repeatedly until you change your criminal thinking.

Relapse is a part of recovery. Keeping in mind the behavioral change model, note that you will find yourself spiraling into this cycle of relapse when you are on the road to recovery several times. If it's going to happen, you don't need to get so worked up about it. You might have to develop a sort of attitude change toward relapse. Consider it to be a building block instead of a big rocky boulder. And don't give up when you face this impediment. Instead, brush yourself off and go because the reward is your journey and struggle.

Relapse is very common when it comes to recovery. The stigma and shame associated with relapse are uncalled for, to say the very least. It is reported that 50% of intensive inpatient programs lasting 4 to 12 weeks result in relapse within the first 12 weeks. If you are recovering from addiction, you should note that relapse occurs in 90% of addicts treated for substance abuse disorder. They revert to their old patterns within the first year of quitting, as reported by the National Institute on Drug Abuse.

While dealing with relapse, you should know that you need professional help. There are plenty of correctional facilities across the states that will help you in recovering from addiction. Apart from that, several Alcoholics Anonymous meetings across the states are very helpful. Unfortunately, since AA is a platform based on anonymity, it's impossible to track the record or recovery rates; however, several people report that they have maintained years of sobriety just by attending AA Meetings.

While it's normal to experience setbacks while on the road to recovery, they shouldn't be common practice. Repeated relapses are not a good sign. If you repeatedly make the same mistakes, you will fall back on the same route where you once were. However, remember the model. You can always start over. One way to avoid relapse is to avoid potential triggers.

Some situations act as cues to behavior. Therefore, you should actively work on yourself and avoid putting yourself in situations that increase the probability of repeating your negative behavior. The best way to avoid doing this is by assessing your life by identifying your triggers. A few common triggers are social settings, emotional states, social-economic conditions, traumas, and dysfunctional family dynamics.

If you develop a positive outlook toward relapse, you'll not get worked up about it. So instead, take relapse positively because it is inevitable, to say the very least.

While assessing your life, you must note that your life will never be perfect. Perfectionism is an unhealthy concept that cannot be achieved. So, salvage the bits and pieces of your life that you have. While you are at this stage, note that you should commit to changing your criminal thinking, quit living two lives, and stop your lifestyle of loners. While it is true that each person should have a unique outlook on life, you simply cannot continue living as a loner for the rest of your life.

Note-worthy assessments are gender and sexuality. Give time to yourself, get to know who you truly are, and if you are someone who cares about your emotional well-being, figure it out. Find out if you are straight, a member of the LGBTQ+, or any similar category. Find what your sexuality is, or at least attempt to explore it.

True change occurs when we change our thinking and attitudes. What has your attitude been like? Have you been lying to people around you? If you are. Sit down and truly write your thoughts down because this needs to change.

Q1.) Describe five life assessment tasks that you complete daily?

_____

_____

_____

_____

Q2.) Explain how you overcame your all-or-nothing thinking.

_____

_____

_____

_____

Q3.) Describe your negative thinking and behaviors.

_____

_____

_____

_____

Q4.) In the midst of you assessing your life and you ultimately relapse, identify who you blamed and why.

_____

_____

_____

_____

Q5.) Is perfectionism a healthy concept that you can achieve? Why or why not? Explain.

_____

_____

_____

_____

Group Activity

Each person has to write what they plan to pursue or achieve in life. Write your goals and discuss them one by one in a group.

To modify negative behavior, you can get involved in the community. Taking steps to join any regular social activity will relieve you from your negative behavior.

Examples that can be included are:
- Religious group
- Volunteer organization
- Sports team
- Professional club

After being released, your friends and family members can help you get your life back together by finding you a list of communities and organizations to help you socialize with your community. Since you will need to have a social group once you get back on the streets, find one where you will enjoy socializing and feel most comfortable.

You need to be able to fit back into the society you belong to. It is very helpful for the convict to envision themselves taking an active part in the social activity of their choice as they find their date of being released closer. If you imagine yourself doing these things, you'll find yourself not being able to socialize more.

If you take time to socialize with your community, you will adjust to life easier than usual. It helps in your transition to life; it helps create a sense of accountability in life. Finding a job can be a great way of rehabilitating and transitioning to real life. Creating a community or joining one can help you socialize healthily. It can even open new doors to opportunities.

Researches show that many people who return from prison find themselves unable to find employment opportunities. So, it's important for you to enter into your old life with a steady job.

Many correctional facilities throughout the states offer programs that are explicitly designed to help inmates find a job as soon as they are released. They teach inmates social skills and interviewing techniques, use computers, communicate with authority figures, and help people sustain jobs. These programs have been beneficial for inmates as they have made them financially stable. Even if there are prisoners who don't have friends or families can make use of this program and have a chance at a better life. Practicing these skills can be done over video conferencing and in-person and can help in rehabilitation:

- Role-play interviewer/interviewee
- Resume writing ideas
- Non-verbal communication skills
- Research potential job openings for the inmate, then prep them with information

Finding employment after being detained is a great chunk of transitioning to society. A series of ventures and non-profits offer placement services and provide resources to companies that hire former inmates.

Below is a list of websites with valuable information on this topic:

- http://jobsthathirefelons.org/
- http://hirefelons.org/
- http://jailtojob.com/from-jail-job.html

Another way you can healthily transition to practical life is by joining a support group. As humans, we are social animals. If you involve yourself in a community where you meet people likewise, you can help yourself get back on track. Ex-cons can help bring your life back on track. Members of a support group can help you identify your behavior patterns and equip you with the appropriate tools to help with the adjustment.

An ex-offender support group can aid inmates in building a healthy and positive lifestyle through their participation. All you have to do is locate the right kind of group. Prior to being released, a person can seek information on support groups with the help of friends and family. Sometimes, the correctional facility staff can help in the preparation of joining a support group after release.

As a newly released prisoner finding accommodation can be hard. Many felons don't have the opportunity of having families and loved ones waiting for their release. Since they don't have much support system, they have to find housing independently. A safe place to live is very important for healthy transitioning. Show that prisoners without accommodation are at the highest risk for recidivism. Unfortunately, most prisoners have no resources to obtain safe housing.

Accommodation for an inmate can be found in the following ways.

First, try and Locate resources by contacting nonprofit groups, local government, and religious organizations that assist ex-prisoners in finding accommodation. On a local level, these groups can provide the best information about housing options available for newly-released prisoners, including halfway houses, shelters, and very low-cost rentals.

You can create relationships by spending time and meeting

with the people who may offer to house your loved one. Then, you can look for tenants that will be willing to accommodate your loved ones on

Completing this self-assessment requires you to reassess your life. Complete this on a separate sheet of paper.

1. Do you lie, cheat, or steal? Start by writing each one at a time and explain who, what, when, where, and why. Then write a solution and what you will do every day to prevent this from happening again.

2. Do you say things about or to others that have caused them hurt or pain?

3. Can you be trusted? Why or why not?

4. Are you always making excuses?

5. Do you think it's crazy to help others? If not, then why don't you help?

6. Are you using drugs, drinking, or overeating? Think back to when you first started. Explain why you felt like it was the solution to your problems at that time. Where and what were you doing? In fact, what were you thinking about and why?

7. Are you prejudiced against other races or sexes? Remember, this is your private evaluation, so don't lie to yourself. Be honest. If yes, ask yourself why. And how has it made you successful, or has it made you a very unhappy and angry person?

8. Do you talk about or make fun of others?

9. Are your friends' negative influences?

10. Do you have a temper?

11. Do other people respect you?

12. Do you admit your mistakes?

13. Can you be trusted?

14. Are you trustworthy?

15. Can you find in your heart to forgive yourself and others?

16. Every day, take some time out to find yourself. Ask yourself, who am I? What makes me unhappy or happy?

Learn to fall in love with yourself.

Chapter 13

Practice Deferred Gratification

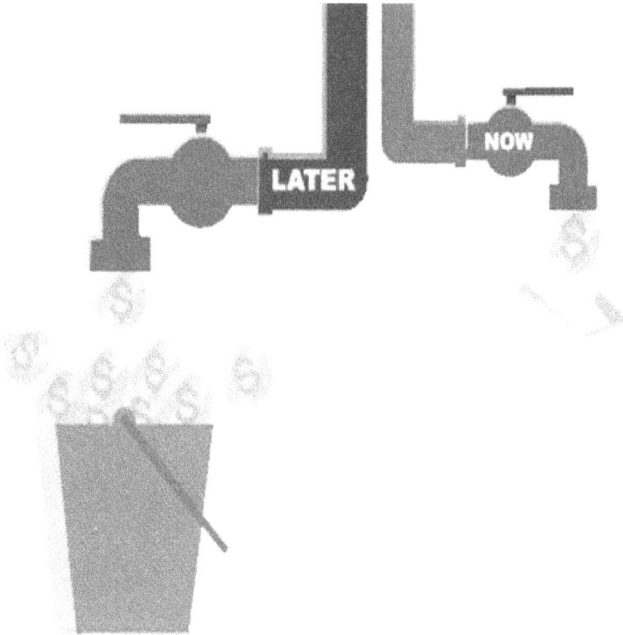

"The most difficult thing is the decision to act. The rest is merely tenacity. The fears are paper triggers. You can do anything you decide to do. You can act to change and control your life; and the procedure, the process, is its own reward."

—Amelia Earhart

In the previous chapters, when we discussed why some people have the tendency to become criminals and felons, the term 'deferred' or 'delayed' gratification was used. This is because criminals or felons find themselves struggling with gratification. They want it almost instantly and can't stand themselves or discipline themselves if it's delayed.

As criminals, we constantly engage in risky behaviors such as taking the law into our hands, acting irresponsibly, constantly bickering with people, and acting selfishly. We also have trouble following orders or rules and struggle to listen to authority figures. When we find ourselves getting in trouble, we make excuses instead of taking responsibility for our actions. This behavior results from conditioning ourselves incorrectly to the environment and lack of delayed gratification.

Gratification stems from the concept of power thrust. It's about trying to control the situation you are in. You have to let go of this constant struggle for power and start letting things go with the flow. You have to note that everything happens in due time. Time is what matters the most. You don't have to get everything now. You can simply wait, and if you can't wait, you have to teach yourself to remain in such situations.

This workbook is intended to help any person who intends to reform their present. As felons, criminals, or a person misusing the law, we often fail to realize that our behavior results from conditioning. As a result, we were conditioned to act antisocial and get in trouble. To remedy this, we must actively take the time to slow down, think things through, become more diligent, and make well-thought-out decisions even if they fail to provide us pleasure or are a source of discomfort.

The road to recovery starts with the kind of decisions you

make. To lead a healthy, happy, and crime-free life, you have to start making good choices. Take one day at a time, and make sure you make good choices all the time. Don't just do something that gives you pleasure. Instead, make a better decision even if it causes you discomfort. You can put reminders on your desk, refrigerator, or even your phone wallpaper. You will not believe the difference a simple reminder like, 'Make Good Decisions All Day" can make.

***

"Challenge and adversity are meant to help you know who you are. Storms hit your weakness, but unlock your true strength."
-Roy T. Bennett, The Light in the Heart

Adversity is a part of life. At some point in life, we all find ourselves struggling and suffering. Tough times are a part of life. And it's not always unicorns and rainbows when it comes to living. There will be tough times, draining times, that will drain the life out of you.

But you have to acknowledge that life is not a bed of roses. Despite being faced with extraordinarily tough circumstances, you have to pick yourself up and continue on the path to recovery. As I mentioned earlier, you are no exception to the rules, and you have to learn to roll with the punches as life throws them at you. And as a responsible person, you have no choice but to make lemonade or lemon tart out of the lemons that life gives you. This approach will help you develop a problem-solving attitude in life, which will benefit you in the long run.

It is quite understandable that you have conditioned yourself to a lifetime of giving yourself chances and excuses that led you to where you are now. However, you need to realize that you have to follow the rules and laws regardless of your situation. You know, you are not alone. The situation, no doubt, can be tough. But you are not alone. You have the whole community, and people have encountered situations like yours before and have gotten out of them stronger.

When you live a life of crime, you are always on edge, anticipating whether you will get caught. Free yourself of the worry and stress and stop being anti-social. Stop acting like a deviant and follow the rules and regulations set in a civilized society. What we achieve in life is an outcome of our choices. So, to live a positive and spirited life, you need to make positive choices.

The epicenter of criminal thinking is around the thought that you think, "I must have what I want and when I want it, and on my terms." However, you must realize that we live in a civilized society and around a community of people. Therefore, we must follow the rules of this society we live in. If you follow the rules of a civilized society, you will be stress-free. As a result, you'll have more time and energy to spend on your well-being and will focus on things that make you happy.

It is important that you understand how valuable it is to achieve something after investing time and energy. Fruits from your efforts are far worthwhile when you reap them after putting time and effort into them. This is a sign that you are now on the road to recovery and reforming your criminal thinking to responsible thinking.

Note from the Author: *The one thing that I want you to always remember is if you continue to commit crimes in the effort to receive instant gratification, you and you alone are choosing to continue living the life of a criminal, and make no* *mistake the consequences will always lead you to incarceration or death. You must seek delayed gratification. It is a sure sign that you are now on the path to recovery. Live Free!*

Examples of Instant Gratification:

Money

Power

Sex

Alcohol

Drugs

Social Media

Food

Q1.) Now, can you name three things in your life that you are at risk of destroying if you pursue them?

1._____

_____

_____

2._____

_____

_____

3._____

_____

_____

Q2.) Can you recall two examples of when you sought instant gratification in inappropriate ways?

1._____

_____

_____

2._____

_____

_____

Q3.) How has your desire for instant gratification affected your life?

Q4.) Can you summarize what you have learned today about the advantages or disadvantages of seeking instant gratification?

Q5.) Can you think of two examples of when you received instant gratification from your hard work?

Q6.) Define Delayed Gratification.

Q7.) List three choices in your life that you choose instant gratification. Explain the end results.

1._____

_____

_____

_____

2._____

_____

_____

_____

3._____

_____

_____

_____

Q8.) How has your desire for instant gratification affected you?

_____

_____

_____

Q9.) How can practicing delayed gratification benefit you?

Q10.) Now, what do you want to achieve in life?

Instant Gratification Deterrent Plan Worksheet

1. Name your behavior change.

_____

_____

_____

_____

2. Name your triggers.

_____

_____

_____

_____

3. Name your avoidance.

_____

_____

_____

_____

4. Name your victories and how you'll celebrate them.

_____

_____

_____

Instant Gratification Reward Replacement

1. Name your behavior and change your goal (Drug or alcohol intake reduction).

_____

_____

_____

2. Name current behavior reward (Alcohol is relaxation).

_____

_____

_____

3. Name current behavior and negative side effects (i.e., heart attack, liver damage).

_____

_____

_____

4. Name a new behavior reward.

_____

_____

_____

Chapter 14

Unstrapping Your Inner Self

"It is imperative you stay in touch with your inner self, so you don't lose the essence of who you truly are."
-Omoakhuana Anthonia

You have made some unfortunate decisions and have found yourself in some undesirable situations. Whether you are in prison, have committed a criminal offense, or are an ex-felon, it's not the ideal situation one wishes to be in. Being a criminal is a choice. In this kind of situation, you have two choices. You can continue committing a crime that will become your identity, or you can choose not to let it define who you are. The thing about defining people by a single choice is largely inaccurate. Yes, people make choices, but sometimes they rely on their criminal thinking to solve the problem. This is distorted thinking. This type of thinking will have you commit crimes over and over again.

It all boils down to one simple question, who are you really?

When you are out in the public eye, you look happy from the outside, but your inner world is often not peaceful. It takes some people years to start listening to their inner self and hear what they want, not what others tell them to do. You have to un-strap your inner self and find out the many layers of the onion that is yourself to get to the inner essence of your existence. To know your inner self is to grasp your motivations, life vision, goals, passion, and fears. It's not what others told you; it's something you've discovered by yourself.

Your inner self knows you better than anyone else because you can only be truly honest with yourself. Everyone is born with a spark; you just need to discover it yourself and follow your passion in life. Here is what you can do to hear your inner voice speaking, reflect on your past, and understand your current self.

To go on an expedition of soul searching to find out who

you are, you must know what your inner self represents and what exactly is a person's inner self-made up of. We carry many identities throughout our lives as wives, daughters, sisters or husbands, sons, brothers, thieves, drug dealers, etc.

These are our identities, but beneath it all, our inner self comprises the values and motives we hold, what motivations drive us to get up every morning and hustle for the day. It asks bigger questions like, who we are as a person, and the values we base our life decisions on. This book is about making good decisions and sound choices to the core. Decisions are based on values that we hold ourselves to and stick to those values no matter what.

We all have to admit that we are more than one identity. Each and every last one of us has three faces. The first face you show to the world. The second face you show to your close friends and your family. The third face, you never show anyone. It is the truest reflection of who you are.

Trying to suppress your inner voice won't let you live in harmony with yourself. A deep part of you will remain broken, demanding changes. Until you stop and reflect on your past, feelings, and future, you actually will not be able to control it. Because your brain is so cluttered, it actually keeps you focused on the past instead of the future.

"Your inner world creates your outer world."
-Matshona Dhliwayo

You can only get to know your inner self better when you are all alone with yourself. During this time, you have to ask yourself some hard questions.

For instance, do you love yourself enough to make good choices for your life?

If yes, please explain why you continue your criminal behavior knowing the negative outcome. Another question you need to ask yourself is who you are hurting the most and why.

Is it your goal to be a lifelong criminal, always going in and out of prison for the rest of your life?

These questions are necessary for you to understand your inner self. You have allowed your criminal self to be the shot caller, the premiere (decision) maker up to this point in your life.

You must address who you currently are to become who you want to be. Get in a quiet place to explore your feelings and understand what causes them. You would want to read, meditate, write down your thoughts, or even cry during this time. At this moment, your brain triggers communication with your inner self that helps you better understand the motives behind your decisions and actions. If nothing changes with your criminal thinking, nothing will change with the criminal consequences that you will suffer followed by your actions, and they go hand in hand.

Did you know that addressing your current emotions will help you find your true inner self? Example: It may be times that you or your family members need financial help and don't have any money; what are you going to do? Your inner self can either solve the situation with your criminal self or your responsible self. Your choice determines your future. Listen to your inner self. What exactly is it telling you to do?

It is proven that you can only get to know your real inner self better when you are all alone with yourself. Many people's lives look similar to yours; they have time for everything except themselves. If you have no time to stop and reflect on your past, your feelings, and your future, you won't be able to control it! Note: A cluttered brain filled with criminal thinking keeps you focused on the past instead of the future.

Here is something that you might want to try when you are so busy having no time for life reflection; why don't you go on a date with yourself? By taking time for yourself, you get a chance to explore your feelings and understand what causes them. It's often challenging to find a place to escape from everyone and focus on yourself. Often, you can engage in deep thinking when you are in the shower or when everyone is sleeping.

Without understanding why you live your life the way it is now, you can't make a difference in your future. Without exploring your inner self, you can't determine what to abandon and what to keep doing in your life. Your feelings are the most authentic reflection of what makes you happy, sad passionate, and desperate. Start noticing your daily mood; it can talk so much about your way of living and your inner self. Did you know that your brain is rational? It prioritizes your pragmatic goals and desires, but not always your personal comfort.

Think of positive ways to go about things when faced with a decision. In previous chapters, we have discussed the many ways to develop responsible thinking, and it's applicable in this situation.

Now, you might find yourself questioning what you must do to find your inner self. The journey toward finding your inner self can be painful and triggering at times. You need to spend time in solitude and do a lot of souls searching and introspection to find who your inner self really is.

Example: By analyzing my feelings, I learned to say "no" to some opportunities that bring anxiety into my life. I admit that I used to be unbalanced with my inner self, but that's changed. I am grateful to God for being able to listen and hear what my inner voice says. You can learn so much by simply getting to know you behind your feelings and past decisions.

"Trauma is personal. It does not disappear if it is not validated. When it is ignored or invalidated, the silent screams continue internally heard only by the one held captive. When someone enters the pain and hears the screams, healing can begin."

-Danielle Bernock

Four ways to start unstrapping your inner self:

Learn to Admit and Accept Your Failures.

The study conducted by two psychologists, Boyraz and Waits, confirmed that thinking about your weaknesses doesn't condemn you to a life full of self-hate. The study also shared that accepting your positive and negative qualities can help you calm your busy mind and improve your mental health.

Overcome Self-doubt.

Psychologist Jennifer Campbell introduced the concept of self-clarity, where she claims that high self-esteem "can be associated with having a clear sense of yourself and knowing who you are."

In other words, when you have supreme confidence in yourself, it is very unlikely that you will continue to judge yourself and devalue all of the achievements you have accomplished in life. Eventually, you will come to a calm place in your busy mind and listen to your inner self.

Cultivate Self-awareness Through Meditation and Mindfulness.

According to Silvia and O'Brien, "self-awareness allows us to see things from the perspective of others, practice self-control, work creatively and productively, and experience pride in ourselves and our work."

Mind the Way You Speak to Yourself.

Researchers made a surprising statement that it's not only what you say to your inner self but also how you do it that matters! So, when having a dialogue with your inner self, don't use the words "I" or "me." Instead, refer to yourself in the third person by using "he," "she," or your name. The research claims using the third person when you talk to yourself can help you reduce stress and anxiety. It can also help you objectively judge your behavior, actions, and emotions.

"Never give up on your inner self! The process of exploring your inner self never ends. It's a journey that you will be on for the rest of your life."

-Perrion Roberts

Finally, we as people are born like blank books, clueless about the world around us, not knowing what the future holds, and trying to find our place in life. We have no idea what will make us happy, who we want to become, or who we can trust to listen to.

All of the life uncertainties trigger negative self-talk that can devalue your self-confidence and prevent you from becoming the person you were meant to be. When your inner self is not at peace, you will all

Q1.) Deep down, with no filters or care for public approval or disapproval, what is the inner fabric of your soul?

_____
_____
_____
_____

Q2.) Why do you continue to have criminal behavior if you love yourself? Explain.

_____
_____
_____
_____

Q3.) Are you happy and fulfilled now? Ask yourself whether it matters what I do in this world.

_____
_____
_____
_____

Q4.) What can you do to eliminate clutter and live the life you want?

_____
_____
_____
_____

Q5.) What do you need to change to improve your current state of life?

_____
_____
_____
_____

Q6.) What would you do if you were not working every day?

_____
_____

Chapter 15

Repairing Your Life and Giving It Direction

"The best way to not feel hopeless is to get up and do something. Don't wait for good things to happen to you. If you go out and make some good things happen, you will fill the world with hope; you will fill yourself with hope."

-Barack Obama

In your life, you have made many decisions that have led you to where you are in life. If your life is a mess, and you have made many mistakes in life, you need not feel overwhelmed. It's never too late to turn your life around. You can always have the life you've always wanted. You just have to have a strong motivation and willpower to turn things around, and they eventually do.

There are plenty of people who have received many awards and medals for their lives and their changes. We praise them for their successes but seldom think about how they got to where they are in life. We will be discussing this further in the book and in this chapter.

"If you're sitting around waiting on somebody to save you, to fix you, to even help you, you are wasting your time because only you have the power to take responsibility to move your life forward."

-Oprah Winfrey

The Unfortunate Life of Oprah Winfrey as a Child – Case Study

The story of Oprah's life is an inspirational one. She was born out of wedlock on January 29, 1954, in Kosciusko, Mississippi, and her parents were never married. She struggled to live in a broken home, where their means were limited.

She had seen poverty in nearly every place she lived. She was sexually abused by her family members, including an elder cousin who raped her at the age of 9. She became pregnant at age 14 and was kicked out of her maternal home.

Besides the wind blowing against her favor, Winfrey managed to turn her life around and dive into the world of public speaking. She was incredibly poor and could barely afford college tuition. Her skill and talent helped her land a full all-expenses-paid scholarship to study Speech Arts at the University of Tennessee.

Thus began Oprah's career in Journalism. She landed her first journalism job at the age of 19 and has only succeeded ever since. Oprah's background and life seemed to go in the direction that nearly anyone of color goes through in America. Despite poverty, sexual abuse, and a thoroughly misogynistic society, Oprah rose to the level where she would be able to host her own show as a Female Person of Color in America in the nineties.

Today, at age 67, Oprah's net worth is nearly 3.5 billion Dollars, making her one of the richest women in America and America's biggest media mogul. In addition, she has made a lot of difference in society through her Oprah Winfrey Foundation and has donated nearly 400 million dollars to charity.

If you think Winfrey was fortunate or lucky, you are grossly mistaken. Winfrey has had a life tougher than most of us. Let's be totally honest. If Winfrey hadn't made the best of the circumstances available to her, she wouldn't be where she is after all those years. The point is, life will kick you to the curb, but you have to get up each time and say,

"I am powerful. I am stronger, and I can do this!"

First and foremost, to give direction and meaning to your life, understand that this is your life, and make peace with it. Accept your circumstances, acknowledge your faults and be okay with them.

You have made those mistakes. You can't turn back time, so forgive yourself and look at things you can do, starting with making changes in your current lifestyle.

You can make lifestyle changes by changing your attitude toward things and situations; if you previously would do drugs, avoid that company. Make better choices and have a better out-look on life. Adjust yourself according to the situation.

Here's a list of how you can turn your life around:

1. Make Better Choices: When you choose, think things through. You are no longer permitted to act without thinking. You will not make hasty decisions anymore. You will be mindful of your choices, and you will find your life turning around automatically.

2. Change Your Outlook Toward Life: Have a more positive outlook toward life. If life constantly throws lemons at you, make lemonade or a lemon tart. Make the most of the negative situations that life throws at you.

3. Don't Let Your Circumstances Define You: Accept your previous identity but don't let it define you. For example, you were once convicted of a criminal offense, but that doesn't make you a convict for the rest of your life. You were a criminal, but that word stops getting power over you when you don't let it determine your life. You are not the same person anymore.

4. Take Care of Yourself: You should take care of your health, finances, and outlook. You are a person who's going to turn her life around. Go to the doctor more often, get a job and save up to move into a better environment. Establish healthy relationships and make those relationships last.

5. Reach out for Help: You cannot turn your life around all by yourself, so establish a healthy support system. You are dedicated and focused on rebuilding your life; make sure that your company around you is as well.

No matter how tough your current circumstance is, you will be able to turn your life around if you focus on this. It's not too late to get the life you have always dreamt of.

You don't have to live in the situations life forces upon you. You can always break free of the circumstances and write your own story.

Q1.) List 3 things that can help you stay on the path of recovery.
Explain

1._____

_____

_____

_____

2._____

_____

_____

_____

3._____

_____

_____

_____

Q2.) How can you make lifestyle changes? Explain.

_____

_____

_____

_____

Q3.) What is your deepest desire?

_____

_____

_____

_____

Q4.) What have you always wanted to be in life?

_____

_____

_____

_____

Chapter 16

Moving Beyond the Guilt and Shame

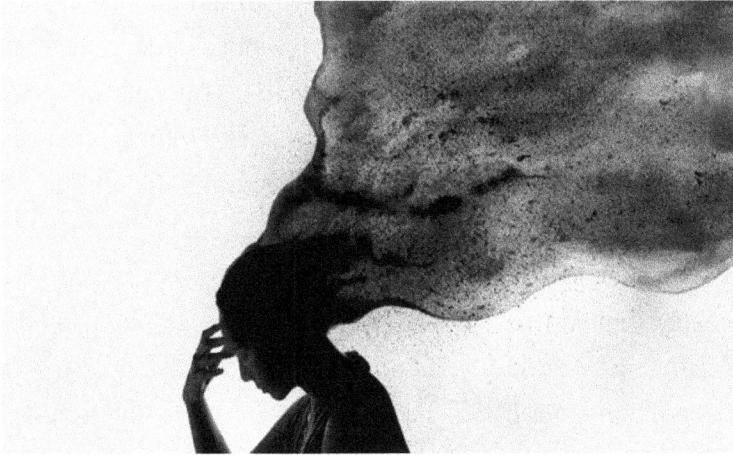

"One of the hardest lessons in life is letting go. Whether it's guilt, anger, love, loss, or betrayal. Change is never easy. We fight to hold on, and we fight to let go."

-Mareez Reyes

Chances are you've dealt with your own internal feelings of guilt and shame. Maybe you deal with them on a daily basis. They leave you with a broken self-confidence and remorse for your criminal thinking behavior that was wrong and should have been done differently. I need you to understand that guilt and shame cause so much damage, and they can be eliminated if people just stop allowing them to thrive within their minds.

Did you know that feelings of guilt and shame are actually a by-product of society's acceptance of the concepts of violence and punishment? Because it could very well be that violence and punishment leads us to view the world through the lens of "right -wrong" and criminal thinking, or it could also be that our criminal thinking leads us to view the world through the lens of violence and punishment.

Either way, guilt and shame are a vicious cycle that is man-made and unnatural. So, how must we find a solution to cut these unnatural and damaging feelings of guilt and shame from our lives? Well, that is simple, you need to stop thinking you're a bad person who has to be punished.

Let me ask you something. Why do you feel you need to be punished? Now, take a step back and ask yourself this question. Why do I have feelings of regret? If you really think about it, would you agree that it's hard to come up with answers to those two questions? But there is a reason why you start to feel guilty and full of shame. It's because you start to feel that the appropriate answer to your self-evaluation is that you know you have done something wrong. Therefore, you feel the need to punish yourself.

We continue to beat ourselves up because we know that we messed up, constantly having criminal thinking behavior. We can't give ourselves a break, so we can't move on. Let me give you something to think about if your child or anyone you truly love did something wrong, but it was just a simple mistake. What would you do to them? Will you continue to bring it up repeatedly, never forgiving them? No, you will not. You will forgive them and extend unconditional love. You will explain to them that we all make mistakes and we don't have to be punished for making them all the time.

"Your mistakes do not make you a bad person. Making mistakes is part of being human. Give yourself permission to release your guilt and shame and forgive yourself."

-Andrea Addington

So, my question to you is, why can't you extend that same love to yourself? You have to stop being so hard on yourself and get it in your head that we all make mistakes. Stop giving in to the social pressure on right-wrong and criminal thinking. It only leads you straight to the guilt-shame punishment phenomenon that continues to promote violence from our neighborhoods to the entire world.

We feel guilt and shame because society has conditioned our minds to do so. We have been conditioned our entire life to look inward at our flaws and mistakes and punish ourselves with hurtful mental thoughts and words. All of this results in those feelings of guilt and shame.

To some, guilt and shame are false feelings that are not real. They are a creation of a cruel and violent society that has endorsed right-wrong and criminal thinking. As long as you are not among those who have committed heinous crimes against humanity, you just have to have more self-compassion and love for yourself and move forward with positive intentions to give yourself another chance to get it right.

Every day, you need to focus on incorporating love, understanding, and compassion into your spirit, rejecting guilt and punishment, and moving past those uncomfortable feelings of guilt and shame ruining you.

In the end, having feelings of guilt and shame takes you away from who you really are and what you were supposed to do and be in life. Once you forgive yourself, you are on the path of changing criminal thinking to responsible thinking.

Q1.) How do you get over the guilt of committing a crime?

_____

_____

_____

_____

Q2.) Why is it important to know the difference between shame and guilt?

_____

_____

_____

_____

Q3.) How have your guilt and shame affected your criminal thinking behavior?

_____

_____

_____

_____

Q4.) Why is it important to know the difference between shame and guilt?

_____

_____

_____

_____

Q5.) Write down everything that hurt you, read them out loud and then take the paper and destroy it.

_____

_____

_____

_____

Chapter 17

You Are Not Who You Used to Be

"Sometimes you have to step outside the person you've been and remember the person you were meant to be. The person you wanted to be. The person you are."

-Mouth McFadden

No two people have the same journey. People have different journeys, and it's absolutely fine. You will find many people in the world. One whose life is sorted and knows where they want to be and others who don't and struggle to find their place in the world. It's okay for you to be on any path.

You have made it till here on the book, which means that you are knee-deep in your journey toward recovery. In your life, whether it was circumstances or yourself that made you pursue bad choices and make bad decisions, you must know that it's never too late to change. You can always move on and not let the hurt and pain of the past define you. You can be your own person, and that person isn't dependent on anyone for their happiness.

You are not the same person you used to be. Remember that you are making changes in your current lifestyle. Adopting new ways to go about things, newer ways to counter troubling situations. This basically means that you are not the same person you were before your conviction.

Now you are a different person. Reinvent your current identity, and don't let your past mistakes hold any more power over you. The choices in your past have had repercussions; they steered the ship of your life in various directions.

But does it have to be the same way?

Does it also have to determine your future, as it has determined your past?

The answer is No.

It doesn't have to have any more power over you than it already has. Become stronger, let go of the past, and don't repeat your mistakes. When you find yourself in similar situations, break free of them.

For example, if you were a drug dealer or an addict, make permanent changes in your lifestyle not to become the same person. Join a support group, quit doing drugs, and avoid situations or people that make you reach out to unhealthier means.

If you were a thief, remember that you don't have to spend your life stealing things; get a job. Of course, things eventually turn around, but you have to believe in yourself enough to know that things will get better, and you don't have to compromise yourself as before. You need to grow as a person to move on. Forgiveness is a beautiful thing that helps people come to terms with their past and present. It also shapes their future by helping them recognize where they were at fault and helping them rectify their mistakes.

It can help you move on and form a new identity.

Once you let go of your old criminal convict identity, allow yourself to reform your old identity into a newer and much more inspiring one. Become a person who's grown and moved on in life. Become someone who has grown and changed as a person.

A person who is no longer a criminal but a chef, entrepreneur, or teacher, whichever path you plan on pursuing. Your life doesn't have to be the same as it has been. You can grow and move on from it. A part of your recovery is forgiving yourself for past mistakes. You must move on as a stronger person who learns from mistakes. Forgiveness can be difficult for both parties. Not everyone will believe or accept your verbal apology; a change in your behavior and actions is the sincerest apology that one can give.

Q1.) Explain what criminal thought made you become the person you used to be. What happened to make you change? Who are you today? Use extra paper if needed.

_____

_____

_____

_____

Q2.)What happened to make you change?

_____

_____

_____

_____

Q3.) Who are you today?

_____

_____

_____

_____

Q4.) Write an apology letter to yourself for your past mistakes. Be detailed and sincere.

_____

_____

_____

_____

Q5.) List the names of those people who you haven't forgiven. (Use extra paper if needed.)

_____

_____

_____

_____

Q6.) List of names of those people who you need to request forgiveness from (The people you hurt). Use extra paper

_____

_____

_____

_____

Chapter 18

Stop Allowing People to Control You

"You cannot always control what goes on outside. But you can always control what goes on inside."

-Wayne Dyer

Being controlled by someone is the worst feeling in the world. You go through life and make choices on behalf of someone other than yourself. This control is causing you so much pain, hurt, and trauma that it doesn't let you move on in your life. So let me ask you a question. Do you feel that you are sometimes in the passenger seat of your own life? Probably so, because now you are starting to notice that you aren't behind the steering wheel, but rather you are a mere spectator looking at life and living your life from another person's viewpoint. If you feel this way, you are definitely being controlled by others around you.

It is very easy to get tired of people controlling you. They think that they know what's best for you. They have to be the ones to approve every decision you make. They feel so controlled over you because, in their minds, they are smarter, better, and more capable than you. To them, it is obvious they should be making and calling all the shots.

Well-wishers or people who seem to care about you are not always the ones looking out for you. Sometimes they enjoy controlling other people, and you can be one of their pawns. But of course, you can see right through controlling people, right? They show you who they are with every move they make. I know it is so frustrating. This type of control makes you miserable because you lead another person's desired life. It can be very frustrating. You will not be in the driver's seat but in the back seat of your own life. You will not drive to your desired destinations but to destinations that make other people happy.

So, you don't think you can make them stop, right? Wrong. You can stop a person from controlling you by taking away their power over you. The question is, are you willing? You don't necessarily have to live this kind of life. Whether or not you think you have the power, you have some authority and control over your life. If you don't want other people to control your life, start by taking back the authority and control over you. It will be painful and challenging because you have been so used to having them make your decisions for you, but it will be very liberating and comforting in the end. So, start by gaining control of your situation, little by little.

If you are really willing to stop people from controlling you, then you need to start looking at yourself first. Yes, you what you are doing to encourage their controlling behavior. One thing for certain you cannot change a controlling person. You can change the way that they see you by giving them a different person (yourself) to respond to. A person with a made-up mind that other people will not control him/her.

Do you realize that you are indulging in controlling people in their controlling ways?

Let me tell you how. First, you tolerate being controlled because you always feel and act like a victim. And what's worse, you are probably not even aware of how you are doing it. When you allow others to control you, it's a subconscious habit. If you find yourself doing it, you most likely learned this a long time ago when there were no options available for you to make your own choices. In fact, one or more controlling people may have prevented you from making independent decisions and learning from your mistakes.

Second, another way to stop people from controlling you is to become strong within yourself. Work on your self-esteem. Research suggests that people who are often controlled and manipulated by others lack self-esteem and are insecure. They let other people control them because they are not strong in their being. So, work on building your self-esteem, and you will see how you are no longer manipulated and controlled by others.

Finally, listen to your inner self and make sure you think things through on your own before making any changes. Follow your intuition and become more in sync with yourself as a person. Anything or any situation that doesn't feel true to yourself should no longer be entertained. You have control and power over your own life, so don't let others control it. Savor it, cherish it and take control of it on your terms.

Q1.) How do you stop giving other people the power to control your emotions?

_____

_____

_____

_____

Q2.) How can you tell if someone is trying to control you?

_____

_____

_____

_____

Q3.) How do you let go of wanting to control everything?

_____

_____

_____

_____

Q4.) Write down and identify your controlling triggers, and write out a solution beside them. Start by practicing saying "No" more often. (Example: If a person makes you mad and you're constantly thinking about it, then that person is controlling you without even knowing it. It is up to you to take control of your own life.)

_____

_____

_____

_____

Chapter 19

It's Never Too Late. Don't Give Up

"Success doesn't come from pie in the sky thinking. It's the result of consciously doing something each day that will add to your overall excellence."

-Nick Saban

Sometimes, we make important decisions and choices in our life. Unfortunately, a good life comes at a cost – constant and persistent struggle. In these situations, the easier thing a person can do is quit and give up altogether. But the reality is that those who quit seldom achieve anything in life, get something meaningful done and achieve their goals.

You have been a person with a criminal record; you have had several convictions to your name or have probably gone to prison as well. Know that you can still turn your life around. It's never too late to do the right thing. It's never too late to make good choices. The fact that you have made it so far in the book shows that you are dedicated to your journey, so don't give up just yet.

You have made it this far, which means you are done with the tougher parts. Deciding to change is perhaps the hardest on the journey of recovery, so if you've made it past this, you just have to push it even further and focus on getting the job done. Quitting midway is the worst thing you can do to yourself. It's like you are quitting on yourself and your goals.

You should never give up on yourself because you owe yourself that much. Don't entertain thoughts that derail your peace of mind or let you get off track from your journey. Remember, the journey is the reward and not the destination. So, don't let minor obstacles and setbacks stop you from achieving the kind of life you desire.

Remember, focus on the bigger picture.

Consistency is key to achieving life goals. The fact that you are here, making efforts to modify your life, shows what an amazing and dedicated person you are. Sure, there are times when we fall and break down but don't catastrophize it. Take it for what it is, a minor setback.

"Rome wasn't built in a day."

Remember, good things take time and effort. When your mind is consumed with thoughts of giving up, don't just repress those thoughts. Talk them out. Whether to a friend, a counselor, or a support group, talk about your fears about your journey. First and foremost, you must come to terms with the fact that it's absolutely normal to have doubts about your journey. Once you accept this, you can move on to the next phase.

When you acknowledge your doubts and fears, the next thing you must do is shape your thinking accordingly. You must restructure your thoughts in a much more positive light. Yes, you couldn't get a particular job because of your criminal conviction. Still, instead of letting it derail your journey, you should accept and acknowledge that it was probably for the best. Have faith in yourself. What's meant to be yours will eventually make its way to you.

If you feel that the situation is not in your hands, focus on what you have control over. In life, there are certain situations that we don't have control over; however, we are not defined by them. Instead of being upset, focus on what you can do when you feel helpless. Avoid negative self-talk and negative thoughts and counter them with positive ones.

Here are some FACTS...

According to Harvard Political Review, The United States has 76.6% of their released prisoners return to prison within 5 years, which means, according to them, you have less than a 25% chance of remaining free for at least 5 years. The odds of staying free are disheartening, but you do not have to become a statistic. Changing your criminal thinking into responsible thinking is the key to obtaining and sustaining your freedom.

Staying focused is sometimes hard, especially when so many negative and criminal things are around you. You must remember that *"You are a changed person, no longer willing to suffer the consequences of criminal and negative actions. You refuse to continue using criminal thinking to solve your problems. You were mentally stronger, wiser, and better equipped to deal with life. You can solve your problems without being a criminal. Never stop aiming toward your life goals."*

"You can't go back and change the beginning, but you CAN start where you are, and change the ending."

- U n k n o w n

Q1.) Write a paragraph to yourself stating how you are willing to commit to change, be specific to the details of your commitment to change.

_____

_____

_____

_____

Q2.) What actions and choices can you make to ensure you will maintain your freedom once released? Be detailed in your answer.

_____

_____

_____

_____

Q3.) What is the key to achieving your life goals? Why?

_____

_____

_____

_____

Chapter 20

Stay Alert. Your Goals Are Manifesting

"Stay focused, believe that you can achieve at the highest level,

surround yourself with others who believe in you, and do not stray from your goal."

-Zach Ertz

On your journey to recovery, keep your eyes and ears open

and stay alert. If you want to achieve something worthwhile, you must be completely focused on yourself. Be fully aware of the situation you are in. The positives, the negatives, and everything else in between!

Manifesting is important in goal setting. To achieve goals, one must set them. The first step toward achieving a long-term goal, such as your goal to leave your criminal life behind, begins with choosing to be calculated with your goals and hence make it a mission to follow them. Manifesting doesn't seem to be working for you because you are over-complicating the process. Manifesting isn't meant to be complicated. When you align with what exactly it is you want to manifest, the better you feel during the process, the easier everything will flow for you.

Resolutions just don't work. How often have you made them, only to give up by February? It seems like every time you make a goal for yourself. You are setting yourself up for disappointment. And because you grew bored and impatient with it, you decided to give up. In fact, fewer people are making New Year's resolutions this year, and guess what? I don't blame them. This is a new year. Let's focus on trying something different?

Ask yourself this question. Why not use the power of manifestation to achieve my goals? Your answer will probably be I do not know how to use manifestation. Well, that is okay. I am going to teach you how to manifest your goals this year by using some simple steps that I have used personally. Believe it or not, I have been able to manifest success in my dream job; I've learned how to manifest more money, attract love, and, most of all, peace. In fact, I use manifestation in almost every aspect of my life to make things happen.

The new year's energy is all about hope, healing, and getting organized, just what we need after a few tumultuous years. This is a perfect time to set goals and manifest what you want! The energy of this year is unique. You need to really take advantage of it by setting attainable goals aligned with your passions.

First, you need to ask yourself, what are you passionate about?

What do you think your purpose in life is?

This is the time for a change, you are going to have to reach out and take this new year by storm, but you need to make sure that your goals are in alignment with what you love and who you really are as a person.

I am assuming that you want to make more money, then think about ways that can align with what you love to do or who you are as a person. And start to live and feel as if you are already living an abundant life. When you start to manifest, try to align all areas of your life with what you want to attract. This includes how you think, feel, and act. It will all come together, and it will happen fast when it does.

If love is what you want to manifest, ask yourself if you are open to love. Make sure you let go of past relationships so that you can heal and move on. You allow yourself to attract love and believe that you are worthy and deserving of love.

The key to manifesting starts with your emotions and raising your body's vibration. Your emotions directly affect your vibrational energy.

This year is about healing, getting organized, and finding ways to be at peace. A lot of energy flowing through this year supports slowing down the pace in our lives while being more mindful and setting intentions with every step you take. Start thinking about your goals and ways to achieve what you want.

First, set goals. You have begun reading this book; it shows that you have chosen to proceed in life. Now, you just have to see where you are on your journey and set goals to move ahead accordingly. Set small achievable goals. You can make a big change in life by setting smaller goals.

Secondly, dream about your goal. Dream about the life you will have after achieving your goals. For example, if your family members don't meet you because of your criminal past, dream about what it will be like when your family finally sees you as the person you are and not the person you used to be.

The third step on this journey is to develop ways to achieve your goals. Formulate an action plan. Devise a strategy on how you plan to go about your life and achieve the lifestyle you want. If you want it, make efforts to achieve it.

While you are at it, tweak your mindset. Develop a much more positive attitude. Trust yourself and know that you will probably achieve it if you work toward it—no need to get distracted. You will achieve it. You are on the right path. If you find yourself on the verge of quitting, use the following affirming sentences to get your eyes on the prize and not give up on your goals.

I can do anything I put my mind to.

I have faith in myself and in my abilities.

I have what it takes to reach my goals.

I can handle anything that comes my way.

Great strength lies within me at all times.

I have the courage to keep going.

Repeat these sentences at least once or twice a day. The

most effective time to repeat these sentences is when you are done with the day and going to bed. You can also repeat these self-affirming sentences twice or thrice a day to help with the negative self-talk your brain might be concocting.

Another great technique is to remember why you started in the first place. When you feel like quitting, make a list of all the reasons why you embarked on this journey and what you plan on achieving from it. List the good that has resulted from the situation and keep on going. Focus on small, attainable goals, live in alignment, and allow yourself to feel good in the process!

Q1.) Write down your short-term goals and place them where you can see and read them every day.

_____

_____

_____

_____

Q2.) What does it mean when someone says they are manifesting?

_____

_____

_____

_____

Q3.) What is the difference between Manifesting and Resolutions?

_____

_____

_____

_____

Chapter 21

Focus On Your Success

"Focus on the possibilities for success, not on the potential for failure."

-Napoleon Hill

Often, people focus on the things they think they cannot achieve. Instead of thinking about negative outcomes, focus on things you have achieved. When you are on a journey as big as this, you will easily get swayed by negative thoughts and beliefs. Therefore, it's important to focus on your successes.

Sometimes we spiral down a cycle of negative thoughts. Those moments reassure us that all good things take time. Just as Rome wasn't built in a day, your entire life as a criminal will not change in a matter of months. Recovery is hard, and instead of focusing on things that you have not achieved, focus on the things you have achieved. Often, people are focused on things that wouldn't go in their favor when in reality, they should be focused on things that could go right.

For example, you have quit cheating and lying because it made people drift away from you. If you don't see your relationships improving, don't stop doing the good thing you set your mind to. Keep on persevering. Keep on moving.

In life, you will encounter many situations that will bring you down. You will encounter plenty of bumps and roadblocks along the way. Remember to focus on what you have achieved and the successes that have come your way. Your journey and your efforts are not futile. They are worth a lot. So, every time you think about giving up, think positive and fixate your efforts on goals that have been attained.

Like most convicts, you have little to cherish about. You have little victories, so cherish the ones you do have. For example, many criminals live and die in their miserable lives and make no change. Consequently, they are thrown into jails and put away for life. You are lucky, and you are fortunate enough to be on the path you are currently on. For you, being on this journey is a victory in itself.

When you are on a big path like this, it's possible to get carried away in the negative wind. When you find yourself derailing, remember that your efforts matter, your life matters. You don't need to get worried or get consumed by thinking that you won't achieve your goals. You will become successful. You just have to become focused on what's achievable and attainable.

Focus on Your Success

The toughest job ever in your life is making changes to your behavior. The adjustments that are required in your life may be very difficult. Over the years, you have developed criminal thinking and acting that have negatively affected the majority of the areas of your life.

As you focus on your success, you need to look at how your criminal thinking has a major influence on your choices. Through this group exercise, you should learn to identify your criminal thinking errors; you will examine their influence on your life and create a strategy for change.

The most common form of resistance in criminal thinking groups is denial. When asked for examples of how thinking errors have caused harm, some group participants will deny that they caused harm to others, or they may even deny having thinking errors. Instead of arguing with the participant or convincing them of the opposite, engage them in a dialogue.

When a group participant denies having thinking errors, consider a response similar to this: *"It makes total sense to me that you don't recognize having any thinking errors. In fact, it actually helps me see why you are in this group/program/ situation."*

When a person makes a statement that they don't have a

thinking error without knowing, it is actually an example of a very common thinking error.

"Do you know which one?"

If they say "yes," ask them to describe which error it is and how failing to recognize errors in thinking is an example of that thinking error. If they say "no," tell them how this is a great opportunity for them to begin the process of identifying thinking errors in themselves that they didn't even realize existed!

Then, instead of telling them which thinking error they are displaying, ask them to read over the criminal thinking error definitions, perhaps as a homework assignment, and identify which errors are examples of failing to identify their own errors in thinking. Creating a culture of positive change within every Criminal Thinking group should be the primary focus.

The following group reading helps support the accountability and victim awareness that most offenders lack at the beginning of the thinking change process. It also ends with a commitment to positive change for themselves and their victims. A group participant reads each line of the reflection, and the group repeats each line in return.

"Crime"

"Crime Hurts People"

"I Will Not Hurt Others Or Myself Again"

As a facilitator, print out the same number of inspirational graphics as group members. If possible, print it on card stock paper, so the image doesn't show through the other side. Then, ask group members to pick a card without looking at the image.

Begin with one person and ask them to show their card and read it aloud to the group. Next, ask the person to explain which criminal thinking error they believe the card represents best and give an example of the error in their life. Then, ask the person to provide an example of a deterrent they could have used to change the thought.

Finally, ask them to describe how the card and corresponding error is a pattern in their life that continually leads them to harmful results. When the group is done, ask them how this exercise can help change criminal thinking patterns and focus on their success.

"Everyone who is successful must have dreamed of something."
-Maricopa (Native American)

Criminal Thinking Patterns:

Closed Channel Thinking:
- Not Receptive
- Not Self Critical
- No Disclosure
- Good at pointing out and giving feedback on faults of others
- Lies by omission

Victim Stance:
- Views self as a victim (the criminal will even blame social conditions)
- Blames others

Views Self as a Good Person:
- Focuses only on their positive attributes
- Fails to acknowledge their destructive behavior
- Builds self up at other's expense

Lack of Effort:
- Unwilling to do anything they find boring or disagreeable
- "I can't," meaning "I won't"

Lack of Interest in Responsible Performance
- Responsible living=unexciting and unsatisfying
- No sense of obligation
- Will respond only if they net an immediate payoff

Lack of Time Perspective
- Does not use the past as a learning tool
- Expects others to act immediately on their demands
- Decisions on assumptions, not facts

Fear of Fear
- Irrational fears (many) but refuses to admit them
- Fundamental fear of injury or death
- Profound fear of being put down
- When held accountable, experiences "zero state" – feels worthless

Power Thrust
- Compelled need to be in control of every situation
- Uses manipulation and deceit
- Refuses to be dependent unless they can take advantage of the situation

Uniqueness
- Different and better than others
- Expects of others that which they fail to meet

- Super optimism – cuts fear of failure
- Quits at the first sign of failure

Ownership Attitude
- Perceives all things, people, and objects as possessions
- No concept of ownership, rights of others
- Sex for power and control, not intimacy

Q1.) Write a short essay about your attitude, behavior, and beliefs. Identify your strength and weaknesses within each one of them. Then write about how you plan to take your strength and move forward in your life and also how you will work on your weaknesses and strengthen that error of your life.

_____

_____

_____

_____

Q2.) Why is it important to have a well-thought-out plan? Explain.

_____

_____

_____

_____

Q3.) Make a list (plan) of your goals (in detail) and explain the necessary steps you must take to achieve those goals. Use extra paper if needed.

_____

_____

_____

_____

Chapter 22

Adjusting to Normalcy and Living Free

"If you look to others for fulfillment, you will never be fulfilled. If your happiness depends on money, you will never be happy with yourself. Be content with what you have; rejoice in the way things are. When you realize there is nothing lacking, the world belongs to you."

-Lao Tzu

The day you are released from prison will be one of the greatest feelings you have ever felt. To be able to return to your loved ones and to the free world is such an amazing feeling. But you need to know that the process of integrating back into society will not be smooth sailing.

You will be facing many challenges, such as not knowing where to begin. The biggest challenges will be trying to reconnect with friends and family, finding a place to live, and finding work, that's just to name a few. All of this can be such an overwhelming process to navigate. This is especially true of ex-offenders who went to prison in their youth. On the other hand, an adult offender at least had some measure of life experience on which to rely. But parolees that have been in prison for their entire lives will find themselves totally lost as an adult in the real world.

It does not matter what a person's age may be. The fact of not knowing where to begin to rebuild one's life is a significant challenge for an ex-offender. It's commonly said that prison changes people. Most people don't realize that having a conviction record changes a person. It changes their mindset and the way that they think. People that have been incarcerated start looking at themselves differently. Whether you were sent to prison or given community service as punishment, you must realize that it's important to develop normalcy after that experience.

To have a normal and happy life after your incarceration, the institution should provide you with the resources that you will need to be successful. This might include reentry training and education while incarcerated, supervision after release, and providing resources to find housing and employment. These are called *"institutional, and community anchors"* by Valera, Brotzman, Wilson, and Reid (2017) and have been identified as a significant component of successful reentry programs.

To develop a sense of normalcy after incarceration, you must do your best to get back into society. As we know, many parolees rely heavily on their families for support and assistance as they transition back to the free world. As we all may know, not many family members will step up to help make that transition as smooth as possible because support comes with a cost.

Financial strain is one of the primary difficulties for families as they try to support their recently released loved ones. It's not just finances that family members struggle with; they often do not understand the "rules" their loved ones must live under. Therefore, they may experience high-stress levels if their loved ones have trouble finding employment, struggle with addiction, or have mental health issues.

Keep in mind there are other factors that can lead to stress in the family relationship that can cause relationships to fracture over time. You will have to educate your family members and try your best to eliminate the stigma associated with incarceration. This can also be done by states improving the communication with family members; therefore, everyone will know what to expect when their loved one comes home. This can consist of your family member meeting with the parole board or post-release supervisors to better understand what is expected of them and their loved ones.

Suppose family members have access to support programs. In that case, contact information for the local workforce office can alleviate some of the feelings of being in this on their own, and plus give your family members resources to help you transition back to normal life as easily as possible.

Q1.) What do I want normal to look like?

_____

_____

_____

_____

Exercise:

On a piece of paper, draw a two-by-two matrix, where the columns are what you like, and the rows are pre-prison and prison times. What did you dislike before prison and don't miss? And What did you like about prison that you miss?

Collect Your Data.

Give some serious reflection to these questions, and commit to complete honesty, especially about what you don't miss from pre-prison times. Be specific about any of your daily toxic interactions, unproductive relationships, and criminal thinking that made you unhappy. Don't settle with something easy, like someone hacked your social media. Go deeper, like the friends you always went with to commit crimes, drink, and get high on all the negative things you have done.

2. Make a List of the Things to Leave Behind.

Some of the things you disliked before you went to prison might not be unchangeable, such as leaving a stressful relationship. Start a list of what you had to leave behind.

Leaving people behind can be somewhat tricky. But in truth, we all have relationships that are simply not mutually beneficial. People all over actually bring out the worst in us all, belittle us, or just bring us down. If your incarceration has been a welcome furlough from these relationships, you should ask yourself whether you can make this break permanent. In fact, this mo ment might be the best chance you might ever have to do so.

3. This Exercise Shouldn't Be All Negative.

Think of things you like while being incarcerated and will miss when you leave. Consider how you might work them into your life after you are released. Maybe you developed your spiritual life, read a lot, or started cooking, and wish these practices could continue. They can only if you do the work. Join a worship group and organize a criminal thinking club to help others change their lives.

Chapter 23

Healthy Relationships Are Vital

unhealthy relationship

Manipulation | Feeling Trapped | Overly Critical | Intimidation | Control | Dishonesty | Disrespect
Blame | Gaslighting | Pressure | Dependence
Hostility | Toxic | Violence | Jealousy
Dysfunctional

"Everyone needs a support system, be it family, friends, cowork-ers, therapists, or religious leaders. We cannot do life alone and expect to keep mentally, emotionally, and spiritually healthy. Everyone needs some sort of support system on which to rely."

-Richelle E. Goodrich

In the previous chapters, we have talked about how this book is designed to serve the purpose of you not ending up back in the system. No matter the crime you were incarcerated for, you are now on a good path-the path to recovery. This may seem daunting at first and appear difficult to follow, but with time, it gets easier.

Let's talk about toxic people. What is a toxic person? A toxic person is anyone whose behavior adds or causes negativity that upsets your life.

The most difficult part of your recovery is to let go of certain family members, friends, and old relationships. Substance abuse toxins are not the only harmful part of your addiction. For instance, drugs or alcohol are bad for your physical health, and toxic people are bad for your mental health. Especially your old friends (aka "homeboy or girl") who were a negative influence and could become one of your biggest hindrances as you are trying to live a crime-free life.

When you have made up your mind to remove toxic people from your life, it will be much more difficult than removing toxins from your body. Actually, you should not feel bad about breaking up these relationships because recovery is all about your ability to negotiate new aspects of life successfully. You don't have enough energy to worry about hurting those individuals' feelings at this point in your life. A word of advice is that it is OK to be selfish, focus on your own future, and continue to change your criminal thinking and behavior.

In the early stage of recovery, it's very important to surround yourself with supportive people. What all this means is your new support network should hold you accountable for any new criminal behaviors. These individuals will help you rebuild your life, not criticize your past mistakes or judge your present decisions.

"Show me your friends, and I will show you your future."
-Matthew Kingsley

Another important thing to note about the path you are on is that you cannot walk alone. Man is a social animal. We need company and people as if our survival is dependent on it. Even in the holy books of Abrahamic Religions, according to ancient Scripture, Adam was alone and isolated in the garden of Eden, and so for companionship, God created Eve. Just like that, man cannot survive alone even if he is in Heaven.

Social isolation can be very difficult to deal with, and socially isolated people experience a lot of stress, anxiety, and distress, often reported in studies. However, social interaction is vital for survival. For example, popular Israeli explorer and traveler, Yossi Ghinsberg, reported that loneliness was the leading cause of his suffering in isolation in the Amazon Forest.

He even reported that he found it difficult to cope with the loneliness and sought refuge in making imaginary friends for survival. Similarly, people or researchers stationed in far-flung areas such as Antarctica or the international space station report that despite the tough working conditions, loneliness resulting from isolation is what they suffer from the most.

Released criminals, ex-felons, and people who have served time in prison or any correctional facility are subjected to a lot of stigma from society. They are subjected to prejudicial remarks and discrimination and often face neglect of their rights. We'll discuss more of the civilian rights of ex-felons in the next few chapters. Unfortunately, this stigma around incarceration leaves little room for ex-felons to socialize and develop healthy relationships.

This stigma is detrimental to your mental health and can hinder your growth if you give in to it. So while this book and your choice to become better will keep you going, you also need a sound support system. A support system will help you bounce back and stay on your path.

If you were sentenced, your family might have also been the victim of people who stigmatize them for having family members in jail. This might have resulted in you severing your ties with your family members and might have also caused romantic relationships to fail. You need to acknowledge that it is absolutely normal for people to experience these. In fact, it's quite common.

According to a paper published by 'The Centre for Youth and Criminal Justice' reviewing the lives of the families of prisoners, imprisonment is not an isolated phenomenon. It brings about a myriad of changes for the person who has been imprisoned and their role in the family. It affects spousal relationships and the bond one has with parents and siblings. The article discusses that prisoners often depend on their family members for financial support and rehabilitation.

So, to restart your life and go on this journey of becoming a better person, you need the support of your family and friends. You should know that family acts as a shield; they protect us and promote our growth. In case you are a part of a dysfunctional family, which is quite common, you should simply not let it get in the way. It would be best if you tried to make your relationship better with them by listening and responding.

However, if it doesn't work out, you should simply accept

that fact and look for relationships to sustain you. These relationships should be different from the ones before. You should be loyal, honest, and giving instead of being manipulative and taking advantage of people like you used to.

Social support is instrumental in recovery, whether it is obtained from friends, families, or support groups. Francis Cullen was the first-ever psychologist to investigate the role of social support in criminal behavior and delinquency in people. According to his theory, support in any way, shape, or form, such as instrumental, informational, or emotional, is linked to decreasing a person's chances of committing a crime.

He suggests that supportive societies and supportive relationships can reduce crime rates on micro and macro levels. This theory goes as far as to claim that social support can be particularly helpful in the rehabilitation of delinquents and criminals.

Identifying Important Relationships.

Q1.) Most of you might recall making family trees while in kindergarten or elementary school. Do the same, but this time, every person, including friends, family, associates, or pets, should be in it. People who you consider most important in your life. Determine if it's a healthy or a toxic relationship.

_____

_____

_____

_____

_____

Q2.) Are you willing to cut toxic relationships? Explain.

_____

_____

_____

_____

_____

Q3.) How do you plan on protecting your path to recovery from negativity?

_____

_____

_____

_____

_____

_____

Q4.) What changes do I have to make?
(Relationships, Friends, Family, Employment, Leisure Time)

Chapter 24

Forming Healthy Habits

"First, forget inspiration. Habit is more dependable. Habit will sustain you whether you're inspired or not."

-Octavia But

Do you often wonder what your routine is like when you get up in the morning? Every morning you wake up and do things without thinking. These can be as simple as checking your phone, going to the bathroom, brushing your teeth, etc. If you notice keenly, you'll realize that you make these habits almost without giving them any thought. No matter where you go, you get up and repeat this pattern. Sometimes, even years go by, and people keep following the same habits.

If you are an ex-felon or have been incarcerated in the past, you must find yourself developing troublesome habits a few times. Whether your habit is smoking, gambling, abusing drugs, or alcoholism, you have to make a change and stop them before they become an addiction. If you are already struggling with addictions, it's recommended to seek professional support while working on your habits. Nicotine Anonymous and Alcoholics Anonymous are by far the most effective groups across the United States. Going to an AA Meeting will help you work on your habits and will help you get to the bottom of them.

We have previously talked a great deal about how important it is to change and modify your lifestyle in this book. Changing your life may sound like a big thing, but it starts with a small step: changing your habits—one habit at a time. For example, changing our thinking from criminal to responsible thinking is not merely enough. True change starts with changing your actions and changing your thinking. It starts when you break the cycle of bad habits and replace them with healthy and positive ones.

What Is A Habit

To understand how we can change our habits, we first need to understand habits and the mechanism of habit formation. First and foremost, the dictionary of the American Psychological Association defines the term habit as *"A well-learned behavior or automatic sequence of behaviors that are relatively situation-specific and over time has become morally reflexive and independent of motivational or cognitive (thoughts) influence—that is, it is performed with little or no conscious intent."*

Habits are automatic and involuntary. They are formed when a person repeats their actions constantly, so much so that it no longer requires any effort on their part. Plenty of psychologists have worked on habits, and they propose that a habit is a response to a stimulus that is strengthened over time by repetition and reinforcement. So, for example, once you receive gratification and pleasure or experience satisfaction, that response is strengthened. As a result, you are keener on responding the same way if the situation arises again.

How Are Habits Formed?

Charles Duhigg's New York Times Best Seller, *"The Power of Habit,"* explains the principles of habits and their mechanisms in detail. Duhigg explains that habit change doesn't occur overnight, so you must be prepared to spend a lot of time and effort to change your habits. And there's also not a set-out formula for habit change that can be applied to everyone and yield the same results. Every person is different and unique, and hence, you'll have your share of struggles specific to you.

The Four Stages of Habits

Cue Craving Response Reward

Popular writer of New York Times' Best Seller Book *'Atomic Habit'* explains that any action goes through four stages to become a habit eventually. First and foremost, there is an environmental cue that triggers a response. A cue can be anything as simple as food, shelter, or clothing to complex things such as wealth, power, peace, etc.

The second stage is the craving stage; it is followed by craving. If your tummy is rumbling, it's a cue, and you will start craving food. For example, you needed money to pay rent before you were incarcerated, which was a cue, and you found yourself craving money. To keep a roof above your head, you craved money.

The third and most important stage is the response. Your response is your choice. It is how you choose to react to the cue. To the core, it is your action; your response is your habit. The response stage is important because it determines what you adopt to fulfill your social and environmental cues. In the earlier example, you can either choose to steal money, engage in theft, scam people or do a dull, monotonous job to earn money.

The final stage is the reward. Your response follows a reward. Your effort will yield results in the form of a reward. It is the fruit of your response. If we consider the scenario mentioned above, your reward would be to keep living in your house. Habit formation is an ongoing process; you will repeat your actions or responses to receive a reward.

So, your response determines the kind of person you are in any situation. When you respond to an environmental cue, you need to implement responsible thinking right there and then. Otherwise, if you choose to respond by not thinking, you'll end up repeating your past mistakes.

These four stages of habit formation occur in a loop. Therefore, it is called 'the habit loop.' It is also discussed in Duhigg's book, 'The Power of Habit.' You can change your habits by replacing your negative habits with positive ones. I'm attaching a few exercises to help you improve yourself and make better choices.

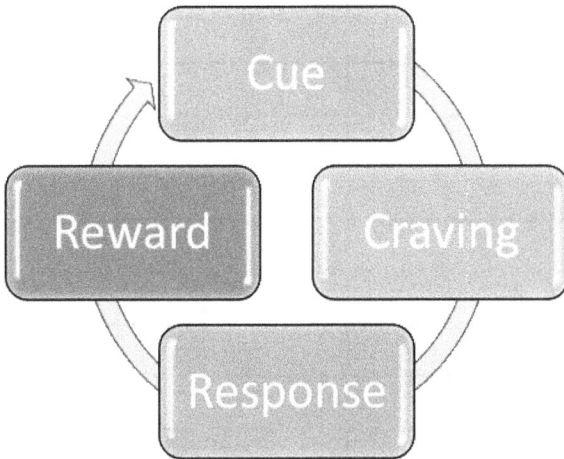

The Habit Loop

Build healthy habits by:

1. Plan Identify unhealthy patterns and triggers

2. Change your surroundings. Find ways to make healthier and easier choices.

3. Ask for support

4. Fill your time with healthy activities.

5. Track your progress.

6. Imagine your future

7. Reward yourself

8. Be patient.

Review Exercise

Can you identify cues, cravings, responses, and rewards from your daily life? As a practice activity, why don't you make a list of your habits from your daily routine?

Mark with a tick if it's healthy and a cross if it's an unhealthy habit.

Cue	Craving	Response	Reward

Habit Replacement Exercise

Can you identify your unhealthy habits? List them down in the order of priority that they need to be changed in and write possible and doable replacements.

Example: Shoplifting à Working extra shifts to be able to afford things you like.

_____ à _____
_____ à _____
_____ à _____
_____ à _____
_____ à _____
_____ à _____
_____ à _____
_____ à _____
_____ à _____
_____ à _____
_____ à _____
_____ à _____
_____ à _____
_____ à _____
_____ à _____
_____ à _____
_____ à _____
_____ à _____
_____ à _____
_____ à _____

Chapter 25

You Are On the Path to Freedom

The key of life Symbolizes the map of existence.
Once you free yourself from all resistance, your path will
Become white- for the remainder of the distance.

- Poetry by Suzy Kassem

We talked about being in an internal prison if you don't free yourself of your habits in the previous chapters. The path to freedom begins first with visualization. You first have to see yourself at the beginning of this path.

When you visualize yourself, you have to decide whether to stand still or start taking steps to lead you to the end. This path is the route to freedom, and it's not an easy one to follow. However, great things await you when you start moving, no matter the speed or rate you are going at.

If you are unsure whether this is the path you should follow, I can certainly put you out of your misery. First and foremost, contemplate whether you truly are unsure, are confused, or are just not accepting your current circumstances. To eliminate uncertainty, you must first be sure that you indeed are uncertain.

If you are, then do tell, what truly is one sure of in this life?

The day we live, the day we die?

What will happen to us the next moment?

Do you think one can be 100% aware and sure of things at all times?

Let's talk a bit more about uncertainty. Consider this scenario. You are sitting in a room full of people. You notice that each person in the room is engaged in some activity. Some of them are eating, reading, or even talking. You know what they are doing, but do you know what is going on with that person?

Not at all.

You don't even know what's going on outside your room. You have no clue what is happening in the world even. It's impossible for you to know everything. Consider your family members, siblings, or colleagues even. You don't know everything that goes on in their lives. You don't know what their day is like or whether they are going through hard times.

Now that we've established that we as humans are absolutely unaware of our circumstances, let's talk about change. You don't know anything about the world, the people who live there, so how can you fit in?

How Do You Change Your Thinking?

At this point, you are probably questioning yourself. You might even be thinking about whether you can actually transition from a criminal thinker into a responsible one at all.

When you feel uncertain about your life, you'll start questioning whether or not there are real answers to the questions that life poses in front of us. You'll even think about whether it is possible to pursue your goals and ambitions according to how it is done because you'll be so uncertain.

You'll question whether you'll be able to fulfill the roles you have as a son, daughter, or productive member of your community. Toward the start of your strenuous and tasking journey toward change, you'll often repeat the phrase *"I don't know."*

Now, to enable you to grasp how you can change your criminal thinking to responsible thinking and help you walk on the path of freedom, you need to become aware of the role you are playing right now. If you think closely, you'll realize that our roles in life are a reaction to our situations. When faced with difficult circumstances or a situation, you have to take charge, assume a role, take responsibility, and react.

However, you act like a loose cannon when a problem arises as you have not learned how to respond to new situations. Instead, you have conditioned yourself to specific responses that you automatically resort to. These automated responses include anger, jealousy, fighting, etc.

When it comes to roles, you have to accept other positions. These roles are those of a drug addict, con artist, inmate, child, or even parent. If you say that these roles don't define you, watch how you react when people disrespect your mother, sister, or child. You will find yourself getting angry about these situations, making you want to fight.

You will go ahead and justify your actions and blame that person. You'll say things like, "They made me do it."

But if you think about it, they said it, but you reacted to it. So whatever they say is meaningless; no matter what they say, it will not change your family or harm them in any way. However, it will surely cause you problems. So you have to learn to react to situations correctly.

Now, you must be thinking, what is a good and bad way to respond to situations or circumstances and what is right and wrong?

You might often question whether you are a good person or a bad person and wonder why you behave the way you do. Hopefully, the path to freedom is not too far. You will be free. You will liberate yourself. But if you really want to succeed, you have to be sincere and honest with yourself.

You have to hold yourself accountable for your circumstances. You have to 'walk the walk' instead of just 'talking the talk.' Now, you will become a modified and much more responsible version of yourself who'll hold a responsible space in society.

Now, after having read the entire book, I absolutely have to make certain changes in my life.

"The future belongs to those who believe in the beauty of their dreams."

-*Eleanor Roosevelt*

Mental Health

"Your illness is not your identity. Your chemistry is not your character."

-Rick Warren

The world is facing greater challenges now than it was before. People all around the globe are struggling with mental health issues. Furthermore, mental disorder prevalence is at an all-time high, with over a staggering 650 million people suffering from mental and behavioral disorders. These disorders are highly prevalent in prison populations.

There are several reasons why mental illness and behavioral disorders are present in prison populations among inmates. First, there is a misconception and stigma around mental health. Second, people consider individuals suffering from mental health as dangerous. However, it is greatly misleading. Neither are they a danger or threat to society nor are they capable of harming the masses.

The real reason these disorders prevail can be attributed to intolerance of certain societies, absence of adequate treatment, in-patient and outpatient care services for patients, and lack of rehabilitation centers. While these factors are important, one of the biggest reasons is the lack of access to mental health services worldwide. According to research done by Sager in 2020, US Citizens with mental illness end up in prison 10 times more than in mental health facilities. This indicates a lack of access to mental health facilities and psychiatric care.

Many inmates and prisoners come to prison with pre-existing mental health conditions which worsen upon incarceration. However, certain prisoners and inmates develop mental health conditions due to their lifestyle in prisons, such as torture or human rights violations. Researchers have coined the term ‘ *Post-Incarceration Syndrome,* ’ a term used to indicate this condition. The symptoms of this syndrome are similar to PTSD, which may develop after prisoners have served their sentence.

According to the psychiatrist, Dr. Seymour L. Halleck, *"The prison environment is almost diabolically conceived to force the offender to experience the pangs of what many psychiatrists would describe as mental illness."*

It is indeed a sad state of affairs for prisoners. Many prisoners who populate prisons across the United States should get the care they deserve in mental health facilities. Instead, according to an article published on the University of Michigan School of Public Health's website, the US Department of Justice holds substantially low standards for prisoners to appear in court.

According to the criteria set by the department of justice, as long as prisoners are mentally sound enough to take care of themselves and carry out basic tasks such as showering, eating, and remembering their name and year, they are approved as mentally sane to appear in court. Unfortunately, this standard is deficient as it compromises inmates' mental health.

Prisons are not equipped with adequate mental health facilities to treat patients. Research backs the statement that there is an absence of mental health units in prison throughout the states. According to an article, Correctional Facilities in the United States, published in the research journal Harvard Review of Psychiatry, the parameters of developing mental health units in prisons are limited. Most mental health facilities are accessible to men more than compared to females. Therefore, the government must substantially modify the existing mental health facilities.

The prison environment is a significant factor that is conducive and promotional to developing a mental illness. Lack of privacy, lack of activities, reduced access to family, lack of peer support, and absence of mental health facilities contribute to mental illness development. Rehabilitation post-incarceration can also cause anxiety in inmates. All these factors collectively pose inmates at risk of committing suicide more than the general population.

People who are locked up often should be institutionalized as opposed to being thrown in prison. Many criminal offenses and felonies can be avoided if these people are given access to mental health facilities. Many people who suffer from substance abuse disorder end up in prisons instead of rehabilitation centers.

It's astonishing how a lack of help can simply put people behind bars for their life. It's not right. They should be treated for their disorders instead of being sent to prison, where they serve their time and get back in once they fall prey to their illness and instincts.

People suffering from mental health conditions face a lot of stigma and discrimination in society. Employers refuse to hire mentally ill people, even if they are high-functioning. Society should develop a more welcoming attitude toward mental illness. Treatment facilities should be more accessible. However, even though there are some mental health facilities, they are not enough to cater to the needs due to a lack of resources.

Even prisons have access to effective therapies and treatments, but they mostly go to waste as they are ineffective, expensive, and limited. As a result, only a few people get access to help. Building a separate psychiatric hospital is expensive to make and maintain and has limited access, so they are not as effective. They also have limited release rates, so they are highly stigmatized throughout the world.

Prisoners released from prisons with existing mental health conditions such as bipolar disorder, substance abuse disorder, and several other mood disorders are more likely to commit violent offenses. Many studies support this fact and have proven that many inmates suffer from major depression and psychotic illness.

At least one in five people that enter the prison suffers from significant substance abuse disorder. Many mental disorders that people suffer from are common and treatable. Suppose the prisoners are adequately screened before release, and follow-up sessions from therapists are mandated for them. In that case, several one-timers may never even come back to prison or harm themselves or others.

While we have established how the system doesn't provide much access to mental health, society is also not too far behind. People don't focus too much on mental health problems as they think that they may re-occur. However, people die as a consequence of being untreated for long. It's high time that the government starts putting in efforts and resources toward prison and mental health. It is not only the constitutional right of prisoners but also beneficial for society as it will improve public safety. People who need help will get it and not end up in prisons.

When treating mental disorders, you have to acknowledge the social and societal factors that accompany them. Many people who have been treated for certain illnesses relapse as they are exposed to the same triggers when placed in the exact same situations they were placed in before. Prisoners must be rehabilitated adequately and treated for their conditions. Mental illness can be caused due to violence. Treatment can bring down levels of crime. However, it is not enough. Prisoners should be given social support alongside treatments and therapies.

The prison, or any correctional facility for that matter, is not a place to treat people who are struggling with a mental illness.

Prisons aren't made to accommodate mentally ill patients or educate people who need them. Therefore, the criminal justice system should not sentence mentally ill patients to prison, and those that acquire illnesses while serving their sentence must be given adequate care.

Addressing mental health issues within the criminal justice system can bring plenty of advantages to society. It has a trickle-down effect. By giving prisoners access to mental health facilities, each and every person in society, along with people associated with the criminal justice system, including prisoners and prison employees, will experience these benefits.

Providing mental health facilities to prisoners can have a domino effect on society. Suppose prisoners are given access to mental health facilities. In that case, the morbid prison population suffering from mental illness and the general population will see a general improvement in the quality of life.

Since treatment will be readily accessible, more and more prisoners will reach out for help, thereby reducing the pre-existing stigma associated with mental illness. If the stigma is reduced or eliminated, prisoners will have less difficulty in rehabilitating themselves in society post-incarceration. If they are properly rehabilitated, chances are they may never go back to prison again.

The lives of prison employees are very tough. After all, prison employees or staff members work in highly demanding environments. With the presence of prisoners suffering from mental illnesses, it can become tough to deal with them. Sometimes the consequences of the behavior of one inmate can have detrimental effects on the prison environment. The job of competent prison management is to create an atmosphere that accepts, responds to, and promotes the sound mental health of prisoners and prison employees.

The community that is present within the prison, including the correctional officers and staff, must all be considered a part of the general population. Therefore, they must not be treated in isolation. Hence, they must have access to all sorts of health facilities accessible to the general public.

The health of the prisoners shouldn't be excluded from public health just because they have been incarcerated. For example, suppose mental health facilities are made available to people. In that case, many people within the prisons can get treated, and those suffering from mental health conditions will get the care they need away from prison.

"The struggle you're in today is developing the strength you need for tomorrow. DON'T GIVE UP."

-Robert Te

How to Adapt to Society After Prison

After spending a long time in prison, reintegrating into society can be challenging and frustrating. You can do it with goals, perseverance, a positive attitude, and hard work to plan and take action. The transition from prison back into society also requires patience. Here are steps you can take to adapt and live your life in the context of society.

1. Figure out where you're going to live. You may already have a home you can return to. If not, ask a close friend or family member if you can live with them until you can financially move into your own place. Make sure the friend or family member does not partake in activities that might cause you to slip back into the former lifestyle that got you into trouble.

2. Take time to think about your goals and aspirations. Then take out a pen and paper and write them down. These might be anything from finding a significant other to starting a career in business.

3. Go through each item on your list one at a time and think about how you can reach your goals. Write a few sentences next to each one about what you plan to do to work toward that goal. Put your list of goals in a place where you can see them every day.

4. Reconnect with friends and family, starting with those closest to you. Tell them you would like to reconnect with them and tell them about your new goals, ambitions, and aspirations. These people can support you emotionally and help reconnect you to society.

5. Create a resume if you do not already have one. Search for jobs online and apply for jobs in your local area that suit your experience and skill set.

6. Go to your local bank and open a savings account. Deposit as much money into the account each time you get paid, only keeping as much money as you need for day-to-day living.

7. Search for housing in a neighborhood with minimal crime and violence once you've saved enough money to pay rent. If you cannot afford the rent of an apartment, try getting a roommate that will split the rent with you.

8. Consider going back to school. If it is your goal to obtain a more high-paying job or a job you like, it may require a higher level of education. This may mean going to community college or pursuing a bachelor's or master's degree. You will need to apply to several schools to increase your acceptance chances. Research schools carefully before you decide to apply to make sure they offer what you want. If needed, you can take out a student loan or seek financial aid.

9. Take up hobbies and interests you like to do in your spare time. It may be playing basketball with friends or getting involved in religious or other types of community groups. Having a hobby and doing activities with others will help you live in the present and make new friends.

10. Let go of the past. Do not let a *"chip on your shoulder"* or anger about your situation impedes your progress. Instead, stay positive, and move forward. Obtain counseling to discuss emotional issues if possible. If local therapy is unavailable or not an option, try an online site such as Prison Talk to help you with issues.

11. Be honest. Most employers will work with you if you

tell them the truth and discuss how you have changed since your experience. Always answer *"yes"* when a job application asks whether you have ever been convicted of a crime. Practice interviewing honestly with a friend or at a local employment agency.

12. Dress nicely, be polite and avoid slang talk when going to an interview. Do not smoke before an interview, and remain drug-free. Make sure you hold the identification that isn't affiliated with the corrections facility you were housed in. Do not bring friends or family members to an interview.

13. Take an entry-level position if it becomes available to you, even if it's not what you want long-term. Stay with an employer for at least six months before looking for another position.

14. Make a list of what agencies offer help in your community and contact each of them to see what potential employment or training is available. Local county job services or job stores can be found in the telephone book under county government listings. Local. Goodwill stores are also known for assisting people with criminal backgrounds.

15. Talk to your counselor or parole officer about what types of jobs you should not pursue based on your crime. If you didn't complete high school, work toward your GED now. Look through your local newspaper's classified ads. Use Internet resources for assistance, including Jobs for Felons, the *"From Jail to a Job Step-by-Step Guide,"* or the National H.I.R.E. Network (see Resources).

General Information
Rights Upon Release

"Your illness is not your identity. Your chemistry is not your character."

-Rick Warren

Voting

First, the United States government believes that all those convicted of a felony must be denied the right to participate in casting their vote in elections. This is called 'Felony Disenfranchisement.' The policy states felony offenses sentenced with a year of incarceration or more or penalized with a fine of more than $1000 are divested to their right to vote.

However, it is upon the court to decide whether the status of the disenfranchisement is permanent or temporary. Sometimes it's temporary, and the right to vote is restored upon completing the sentence.

The United States is perhaps the most stringent country regarding declining felons' right to vote. Therefore, you need to take your criminal convictions seriously. The United States' constitution denies those who fail to respect the laws of a civilized community to participate in important decisions that concern it. Many people advocate that criminals shouldn't have any say in political decisions as they don't respect the state's laws anyway.

In 2018, after a lot of advocacy and awareness, the US government allowed previously convicted criminals the privilege to cast their vote upon completion of their sentence. As a result, today, not many states implement permanent felony disenfranchisement, and it's limited to states including Florida, Iowa, Kentucky, and Virginia.

However, a few states restrict the right to vote based on 'Moral turpitude.' These are felons convicted of cases that shock the public conscience, such as aggravated assault, voluntary manslaughter, kidnapping, etc.

Today, many states in the United States allow ex-felons or people who've completed their sentence the right to vote. Iowa has re-enfranchised hundreds of thousands of ex-felons, giving them the right to vote. In addition, the State of Iowa allows people to vote upon completing their sentence, popularizing the concept of felony disenfranchisement.

Back in 2018, the state of Florida amended the constitution, giving ex-felons the chance to vote again after completing their sentences, excluding those convicted of cases of moral turpitude. This amendment proved to be monumental in the history of prison rights.

However, the Republicans passed a law that instated that all ex-felons convicted besides moral turpitude should clear their court dues before being granted the right to vote. Unfortunately, this move denied thousands of US Citizens in Florida the right to vote, as many people found themselves unable to clear their upstanding dues. It is, however, being challenged in court, and plenty of federal rulings are inclining toward it in favor of legalizing it.

The trend toward giving felons the right to vote is receiving much acclaim, and the movement is gaining mass momentum. Many people advocate that felons be permitted to exercise their right to vote after completing their sentence. Several activists believe that every US Citizen deserves to be granted a right to vote despite the felony committed and even extend their advocacy to those currently incarcerated. Maine and Vermont permit prisoners to exercise their right to vote even from prisons, no matter the kind of violation perpetrated by them.

Apart from these states, many states sanction people and refute felons to exercise their right to vote partially or wholly, including partial disenfranchisement for felons upon completion of their sentence or post probation or parole. In addition, felons convicted of cases of moral turpitude are denied the right to vote permanently.

Activists that counter felony disenfranchisement believe that every US Citizen should be granted the right to vote, despite having a felony record or offense. Further, they argue that the criminal justice system in-differentially influences racial minorities, predominantly African-American people and people of color, thereby implementing felony disenfranchisement, which marginalizes them further by denying them their rights.

Can ex-felons vote in your state?

States can let ex-felons vote in prison, after probation, parole, or prison, or never

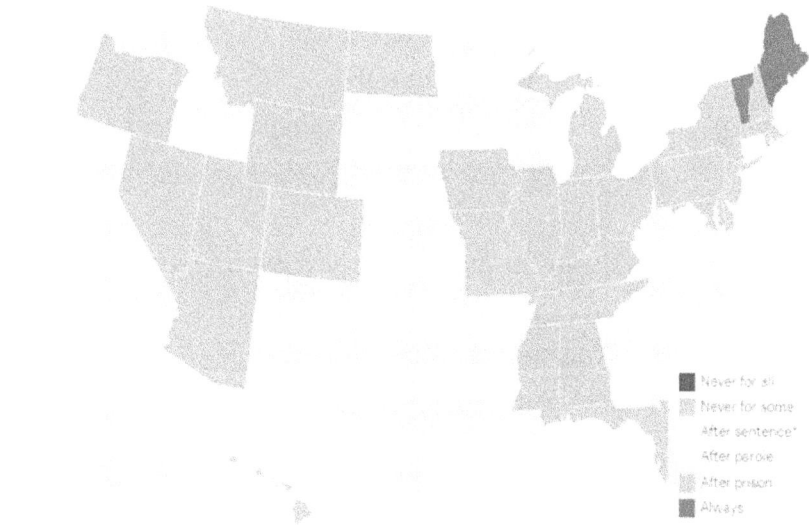

Never for all
Never for some
After sentence*
After parole
After prison
Always

*Includes probation, parole, and prison time.
Source: Brennan Center for Justice

Vox

Some people go as far as to argue that this systematic neglect is intentional and dates back to the racially segregated

America of the Jim Crow Era, replacing racial segregation with legalizing the systematic oppression of minorities by purposefully passing laws that wrote off people of color. As a result, allowing felons to vote receives a lot of hostility in states where it is amended in the constitution, such as the state of Florida.

Many people argue that the opposition to the resistance to felony disenfranchisement is largely political. It is speculated that permitting ex-felons the right to vote will increase the public acclaim and popularity of the democrats. Another argument from people who support felony disenfranchisement suggests that refuting felons' right to vote is a form of punishment and can motivate people not to commit federal offenses.

The conflict and dispute following it are not limited to dialogue and conversation between republicans only and are also discussed in the Democratic Party. For example, Senator Bernie Sanders of the Democratic Party argued that people should be allowed to participate in elections from prisons. In 2016, a staggering 6 million Americans failed to participate in elections due to felony convictions.

This huge number impacted the results greatly, including denying nearly 20% of African-American voters in Kentucky, Tennessee, Florida, and Virginia. It is argued that even though not every single person is guaranteed to vote, denying them their right to vote could mean a decrease in numbers of Democratic voters as a lot of minorities favor democrats as opposed to republicans.

It could mean bad news for states with very close numbers, including Florida. The 2020 Presidential Elections could have had different outcomes if felons hadn't been stripped of their right to vote and become disenfranchised.

State Felon Voting Laws and Policies

Some states, like Virginia, have laws on the books that contradict current state policy as enacted by the current governor. Here we have tried to list the current policy as it impacts those with felony convictions. 9 States may lose the right to vote permanently.

Alabama, Arizona, Delaware, Florida, Iowa, Kentucky, Mississippi, Tennessee, and Wyoming.

Maryland and Missouri may permanently disenfranchise voters convicted of certain election crimes, but we've categorized the states according to the policy for the most people.

16 States restored after Prison, Parole, and Probation

Alaska, Arkansas, Georgia, Idaho, Kansas, Minnesota, Missouri, Nebraska, New Mexico, Oklahoma, South Carolina, South Dakota, Texas, West Virginia, and Wisconsin

2 States Vote Restored after Prison and Parole Connecticut and Louisiana

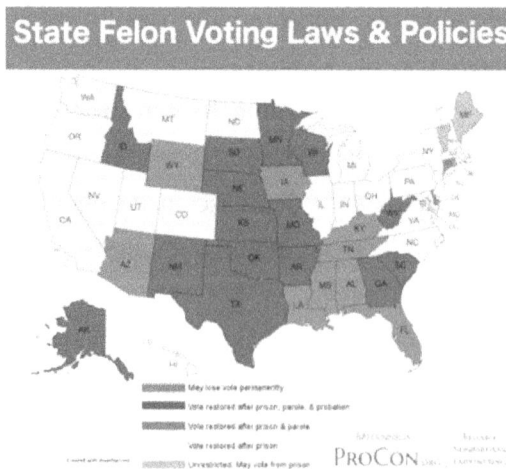

State Felon Voting Laws & Policies

21 States: Vote Restored After Prison

California, Colorado, Hawaii, Illinois, Indiana, Maryland, Massachusetts, Michigan, Montana, Nevada, New Hampshire, New Jersey, New York, North Carolina, North Dakota, Ohio, Oregon, Pennsylvania, Rhode Island, Utah, Virginia, and Washington.

The Washington legislation signed on Apr. 712021 by Governor Jay Inslee restoring the right to vote upon release from prison goes into effect in Jan. 2022. Until then, the right to vote is not restored until prison, parole, and probation are completed.

2 states and DC: Unrestricted; May Vote from Prison

DC, Maine and Vermont

Alabama

Some people convicted of a felony may apply to have their vote restored immediately upon completing their full sentence. However, those convicted of certain felony offenses such as murder, rape, incest, sexual crime against children, and treason are not eligible for re-enfranchisement.

Instructions for Voting Restoration, State of Alabama (accessed Oct. 24, 2017)

Arizona

Automatic voting restoration upon completion of sentence and payment of all fines for first-time, single-felony offenders. Second-time felony offenders may apply for restoration with their county after the completion of their sentence.

Instructions for Voting Restoration, State of Arizona, (accessed Oct. 24, 2017)

California

On Sep. 28, 2016, California Gov. Jerry Brown signed AB 2466, a bill that allows convicted felons serving time in county jails (rather than state prison) to vote from within the jail.

On Nov. 3, 2020, California voters approved Proposition 17, allowing people on parole to vote.

Assembly Bill No. 2466 (accessed Oct. 4, 2016)

Ballotpedia, "California Proposition 17, Voting Rights Restoration for Persons on Parole Amendment," ballotpedia.org (accessed Nov. 4, 2020)

Colorado

On July 1, 2019, a law went into effect that enfranchises people convicted of felonies who have been released from prison but who are serving parole.

Source: Alex Burnes, "As of Today, 11,467 Colorado Parolees Can Register to Vote. Will They?" coloradoindependent.com, July 2019

Florida

On Nov. 6, 2018, Florida voters passed Amendment 4 (64% in favor - 36% opposed), allowing people with prior felony convictions (other than murder and sex offenses) to automatically regain their ability to vote once they have served their terms of incarceration and completed all parole and probation. On June 28, 2019, Governor Ron DeSantis signed bill SB 7066, which requires former felons to pay all restitution, court fees, and fines before regaining the right to vote.

The law has since undergone several rounds of court challenges. The US Supreme Court ruled on July 16, 2020, that the state of Florida can enforce the law requiring payment of fines prior to restoration of voting rights. On Sep. 11, 2020, the 11th Circuit Court of Appeals upheld the Florida law requiring payment, stating, "Florida withholds the franchise from any felon, regardless of wealth, who has failed to complete any term of his criminal sentence—financial or otherwise."

Sources: The Washington Post, "Florida Passes Amendment to Restore Felons' Voting Rights," washingtonpost.com, Nov. 7, 2018

Brooke Seipel, "Florida Gov Signs Law Requiring Felons to Pay Off Fines before They Can Vote," thehill.com, June 28, 2019

Tal Axelrod, "Florida Supreme Court Rules Convicted Felons Must Pay Fines, Fees before Voting," thehill.com, Jan. 16, 2020

Tal Axelrod, "Court Sides with Ex-Felons Who Challenged Florida Voting Requirement," the hill.com, Feb. 19, 2020

Lori Rozsa, "Federal Judge Expands Voting Decisions to Apply to All Ex-Felons in Florida," washingtonpost.com Apr. 7, 2020

Corey Goldstone, "Ruling at Upcoming Trial Will Apply to Hundreds of Thousands of Floridians Seeking Voting Rights Restoration," campaignlegal.org, Apr. 7, 2020

Lawrence Mower, "Appeals Court Halts Florida Felons from Registering to Vote, Pending further Review," miamiherald.com, July 1, 2020

Dan Berman, "Supreme Court Says Florida Can Enforce Law Limiting Felons Who Owe Fines from Voting," cnn.com, July 16, 2020

J. Edward Moreno, "Court Upholds Florida Law Requiring

Felons to Pay Fines, Fees before They Can Vote," thehill.com, Sep. 11, 2020

According to the Florida Rights Restoration Coalition website (accessed Nov. 7, 2018), "If you were convicted of a felony in another state and had your civil rights restored before you became a Florida resident, you do not need to apply for RCR [restoration of civil rights] in Florida."

Iowa

On Jan. 14, 2011, the Republican Governor of Iowa, Terry Branstad, issued executive order 70, rescinding a law allowing people convicted of a felony to automatically have their ability to vote restored after completing their sentences. The automatic voting restoration law had been instituted by former Democratic Governor Tom Vilsack's signing of executive order 42 in 2005. Felons in Iowa must now pay all outstanding monetary obligations to the court in addition to completing their sentence and period of parole or probation. People convicted of a felony may then apply to restore the ability to vote.

On Aug. 5, 2020, Iowa Governor Kim Reynolds signed an executive order automatically restoring the vote to former felons who have completed their sentences. However, people convicted of felony homicide will still have to apply for re-enfranchisement.

Executive Order 70 - Signed Jan. 14, 2011, Terry Branstad, Governor (R)

Branstad, Governor (R) Executive Order 42 — Signed July 4, 2005, Thomas J. Vilsack, JD, Governor (D) Iowa Streamlined Application for Restoration of Citizenship Rights (accessed Oct. 20, 2017) Veronica Stracqualursi, "Iowa Governor Signs Executive Order Restoring Some Ex-Felons' Voting Rights," cnn.com, Aug. 5, 2020

Kentucky

On Nov. 24, 2015, Kentucky Gov. Steven L. Beshear issued executive order 2015-871 to automatically restore the right to vote to nonviolent felons who have completed probation and parole and have no outstanding court-ordered restitution payments. On Dec. 22, 2015, newly elected Gov. Matthew G. Bevin issued executive order 2015-052, rescinding the previous Governor's executive order. On Dec. 12, 2019, on his third day in office, newly elected Gov. Andy Beshear (son of former governor Steven Beshear) signed an executive order restoring the vote to 140,000 people who had completed their sentences for nonviolent felonies.

Those convicted of violent felonies did not have their votes restored, leaving Kentucky categorized as a state where people may permanently lose their votes.

Executive Order 2019-033 — Signed Dec. 12, 2019, Andy Beshear. Governor D

Executive Order 2015-052 — Signed Dec. 22, 2015, Matthew G. Bevin, Governor (R) Executive Order 2015-871 — Signed Nov. 24, 2015, Steven L. Beshear, Governor (D) Kentucky Application for Restoration of Civil Rights (accessed Oct. 24, 2017)

Louisiana

On May 31, 2018, Louisiana Gov. John Bel Edwards signed House Bill 265 into law. Once the law goes into effect on Mar. 1, 2019, all people who have been convicted of a felony in Louisiana and who have not been incarcerated in prison during the previous five years will be allowed to register to vote, even if they are still serving a term of probation or parole.

House Bill 265 - Signed May 31, 2018, John Bel Edwards, Governor (D)

Maryland

On Feb. 9, 2016, the Maryland General Assembly overrode the Governor's veto of SB 340 and restored the vote to all convicted felons immediately upon their release from prison. Previously, convicted felons in Maryland had to complete all parole and probation before they were able to vote.

Senate Bill 340 (accessed Feb. 9, 2016)

Mississippi

People convicted of a felony are barred from voting only if they have been convicted of one or more of the following specific felony crimes:

"Murder, rape, bribery, theft, arson, obtaining money or goods under false pretense, perjury, forgery, embezzlement, bigamy, armed robbery, extortion, felony bad check, felony shoplifting, larceny receiving stolen property, robbery, timber larceny, unlawful taking of a motor vehicle, statutory rape, carjacking, or larceny under lease or rental agreement."

To regain the ability to vote, an individual, after completion of his/her sentence, must go to his/her state representative and convince them to author a bill restoring the vote to that individual personally. Both houses of the legislature must then pass the bill. Re-enfranchisement can also be granted directly by the governor.

Individuals convicted of felonies in Mississippi remain eligible to vote for US President in federal elections.

Mississippi Constitution: Article 12, Section 241 (accessed June 8, 2012) Mississippi Constitution: Article 12, Section 253 (accessed June 8, 2012)

Nebraska

People convicted of a felony are automatically permitted to vote two years after completion of their sentence of incarceration and all parole and probation for all convictions except treason.

Felon Voting Rights FAQ (accessed Oct. 24, 2017)

Nevada

On May 30, 2019, Nevada's governor signed Assembly Bill 431, which allowed for the automatic restoration of voting privileges to all people upon release from prison.

Nevada Assembly Bill 431 (accessed May 30, 2019)

New Jersey

On Dec. 18, 2019, Governor Phil Murphy signed legislation to restore voting rights to those on probation or parole after completing prison sentences. The law will take effect in Mar. 2020. Previously, voting was allowed only after completion of probation or parole.

Source: Reid Wilson, "New Jersey Governor Signs Voting Rights Restoration Bill," thehill.com, Dec. 18, 2019

New York

On Apr. 18, 2018, New York Governor Andrew Cuomo issued Executive Order 181 to restore the right to vote to parolees, dependent upon a review of records by the Governor's Office. Accordingly, the Commissioner of the Department of Corrections and Community Supervision will submit records for individuals released from prison in the prior month beginning on May 1, 2018, for review. Previously, voting was allowed only after the completion of parole.

On May 4, 2021, Governor Cuomo signed a bill into law that automatically restores voting rights upon release from prison, even if the person is on parole. Previously, under Cuomo's executive order, the person would have to apply for a review of records.

Executive Order No. 181, Signed Apr. 18, 2018, Andrew M. Cuomo

Jordan Williams, "Cuomo Signs Legislation Restoring Voting Rights to Felons upon Release from Prison," thehill.com, May 5, 2021

North Carolina

On Aug. 23, 2021, a three-judge panel in North Carolina issued a preliminary injunction declaring that people convicted of felonies who have completed their prison time must be allowed to register to vote immediately. The injunction restored the right to vote to about 56,000 people who are on probation, parole, or post-release supervision. The injunction may be appealed.

Associated Press, "Roughly 56,000 Felony Offenders Can Now Vote In North Carolina," npr.org, Aug. 23, 2021

Mychael Schnell, "Civil Rights Groups: North Carolina Ruling Will Allow 56K Felony Offenders to Vote," thehill.com,

Aug. 23, 2021

South Dakota

On Mar. 19, 2012, HB 1247 was enacted. The bill took the ability to vote away from convicted felons serving terms of probation. Previously, only people on parole or incarcerated were ineligible to register to vote. Now convicted felons must serve their full term of incarceration, parole, and probation before they may register to vote.

South Dakota: HB 1247 (accessed June 8, 2012)

Tennessee

All people convicted of a felony since 1981, except for some serious felonies such as murder, rape, treason, and voter fraud, may apply to the Board of Probation and Parole for voting restoration upon completion of their sentence.

People convicted of a felony between Jan. 15, 1973, and May 17, 1981, are eligible to register to vote regardless of the crime committed. However, people convicted of certain felonies prior to Jan. 15, 1973, may be barred from voting.

Tennessee Restoration of Voting Rights (accessed Oct. 24, 2017)

Virginia

Virginia law indicates that former felons will be disenfranchised.

On Apr. 18, 2014, Governor Terry McAuliffe announced changes to Virginia's restoration of rights process. Under the new rules, people convicted of non-violent felonies (including drug crimes) will have their ability to vote automatically restored, providing that they:

1. Have completed their term of incarceration and all probation or parole; 2. have paid all court costs, fines, and any restitution; and 3. have no pending felony charges.

On June 23, 2015, Governor McAuliffe announced that *"outstanding court costs and fees will no longer prohibit an individual from having his or her rights restored."*

On Apr. 22, 2016, Governor McAuliffe signed an order restoring the vote to all 200,000+ felons Fredreka Schouten, "Virginia Gov. Northam Restores Voting Rights to 69,000 Former Felons with New Policy," cnn.com, Mar. 16, 2021, Governor McAuliffe's Statement on the Virginia Supreme Court Decision (accessed July 26, 2016) Governor McAuliffe Restores Voting and Civil Rights to Over 200,000 Virginians (accessed Apr. 22, 2016) Governor McAuliffe Announces New Reforms to Restoration of Rights Process (accessed July 2, 2015) Governor McAuliffe's Letter Outlining His Policy Changes (accessed Apr. 21, 2014)

Washington

All people with a felony conviction must re-register to vote after completing their sentence and all parole and probation. However, the Secretary of State's website states that "your voting rights can be revoked if the sentencing court determines that you have failed to comply with your legal, financial obligations."

Legislation signed on Apr. 7, 2021, by Governor Jay Inslee restores the right to vote upon release from prison and goes into effect in Jan. 2022. Until then, the right to vote is not restored until prison, parole, and probation are completed.

Felons and Voting Rights (accessed Oct. 20, 2017)

Wyoming

Effective July 1, 2017, W.S. §7-13-105 allows individuals convicted of first-time nonviolent felons to automatically have their right to vote restored if they completed their supervision or were discharged from an institution on or after January 1, 2010. Individuals who completed their sentence prior to January 1, 2010, must apply for restoration of the right to vote. All others convicted of a felony must be pardoned or have their rights restored by the governor.

Wyoming Restoration of Voting Rights (accessed Oct. 24, 2017) Wyoming Restoration of Voting Rights Application (accessed Oct. 24, 2017)

Rebuilding Prisoners and Returning Citizen's Credit

Success in life requires training, discipline, and hard work.

The United States is starting to acknowledge the gross inequities in our criminal justice system. There are currently over 2.2 million individuals incarcerated in the US today, and 60 percent of them are Blacks and Latinos. Today, more than 650,000 individuals return to society from federal and state prisons each year, and this number is expected to rise with the new reform.

However, myriad barriers make it hard for returning citizens—formerly incarcerated individuals—to integrate back into society. These barriers include being denied housing and employment and are compounded by paying outstanding court fees and other bills.

If you don't have a job, you can't pay these bills. But how do you get a job? Is it as simple as having the technical skills or job training? No—there are still barriers like *'checking the box'* that asks if you have a criminal record.

But is it as simple as just banning the box, then?

No, because while some states have made this decision, we still see significant numbers of returning citizens in these states being denied access to employment. Banning the box is just one barrier—not the only barrier.

Credit is the hidden elephant in the room that we seldom consider when we think about supporting returning citizens. Yet, it is a factor that we must address to help eliminate some of the immediate burdens that returning citizens face upon being released.

Why should we be thinking about credit for returning citizens?

How important can credit really be?

And don't they have bigger things to worry about than credit?

These are really important questions that can be answered by turning our attention to what's happening when an inmate is in custody. They are not an active member of society and therefore is not keeping their finances active. Without renting an apartment, using a credit card, or paying utility bills, inmates have no opportunities to build or even establish credit.

More often than not, this financial inactivity contributes to sharp declines in credit for the incarcerated population. In addition, most inmates have bills that become outstanding during their time in custody, and these bills often end up going to collections. So, more often than not, former inmates return to society with very low credit or no credit at all.

In a society where credit is the doorway to opportunity, having poor or no credit can prove detrimental.

According to a study by the FDIC, let's think about the population that is disproportionately represented in these institutions—people from low-income backgrounds and communities of color—a population with the highest unbanked rates. This means that when inmates enter jail or prison, most of them already live on the fringes of the financial mainstream and walk in with poor credit.

Once released, returning citizens must pay court fees and other bills like child support and find secure housing. To cover these expenses, returning citizens would need to get a job that can generate enough income—but since many individuals are denied employment due to poor credit history, getting a job is an uphill battle.

When the three out of the four major things that former inmates need (employment, housing, debt-reduction, and counseling) to meet these legal obligations are in some way contingent on credit, and many returning citizens have poor or no credit, then it is understandable why many former inmates recidivate.

I would advocate integrating credit building into reentry programming upon release and while inmates are still incarcerated. Helping inmates establish good credit while incarcerated, or at the very least, teaching them how to improve their credit after release, will help to jumpstart their success.

I am working on programs to improve the credit of financially vulnerable individuals; therefore, at the end of the program, individuals will be able to use their improved credit scores to get jobs and move into higher-quality apartments. In addition, if credit building were offered during incarceration and the reentry process, returning citizens would have a chance to improve their credit scores and maximize the payoff of the job training offered in reentry programs.

Without integrating credit-building during incarceration and reentry, returning citizens risk only receiving short-term successes, such as acceptance into transitional housing without securing a permanent place to live and not achieving long-term financial stability.

Employment

Post-incarceration rehabilitation can be very tough. We have talked about how you need to get your life sorted out after being released from prison or after completing your sentence. In most cases, you'll find that finding a job will be extremely difficult if you have a felony record. In addition, you'll find it challenging to secure a job because many employers fear recruiting a person convicted of a crime as they believe that they won't be reliable employees. However, this is a far stretch from the truth.

Unfortunately, it hasn't changed major public perception of ex-felons. Having no criminal record is a prerequisite for many jobs throughout the states. A felony record may delay the job acquisition prospect post-release; however, employment eventually comes around. In addition, several Federal laws protect ex-felons against hiring discrimination by employers.

These laws ensure equality and justice among people in America by granting access to employment opportunities for every single person. They instate that no one should be deprived of employment opportunities unnecessarily and every person be given a chance to be financially self-sufficient.

The Federal Law Title VII of the Civil Rights Act of 1964 forbids private employers to discriminate against people against race, the color of skin, religion and belief system, and nationality. The Supreme Court further states that Title VII of the civil rights negates any employment practice that is seemingly neutral but unfairly impacts a racial minority due to prejudice until or unless the employer can establish grounds for it being a business necessity.

Even though Federal Law Title VII doesn't extend its protection to ex-felons, the Equal Employment Opportunity Commission (EEOC) interprets that discrimination based on conviction extends, showing disparity toward ethnic minorities. In addition, it means that the employer cannot deny you employment based on your conviction unless it's a 'business necessity.

Now, let's discuss how employers can establish a 'business necessity.' If the employer is refuting the right to a job, you must show how the conviction is directly linked to the job you are applying for. The important factors to be considered while determining whether it is a business necessity not to recruit someone with a conviction include:

The kind of offense committed by the criminal

The amount of time passed since the conviction or the completion of the sentence

The kind of job that the ex-con is seeking

Take the example of a person applying for the job of an automobile driver. That person was convicted of a *'driving under the influence'* charge. While they can apply to jobs that don't require driving, the chances of being hired will be slim. A person convicted of theft won't be allowed a cashier's job. Convictions that demonstrate that you are an unreliable or dangerous person can limit your opportunities for certain jobs.

The EEOC Title VII is also interpreted in that it prohibits the exclusion of previously convicted criminals if a justified business necessity is absent. However, it can be very difficult to claim employment discrimination on the employers' part. To prove such a claim, you will have to establish how the hiring practice has disproportionately impacted a protected class such as an ethnic or racial minority.

Suppose you effectively establish a prima facie case (a justified presumption on face value). In that case, the employer has to prove that refuting you the right to the job aligns with a business necessity. Let's assume that the employer successfully demonstrates that hiring you directly conflicts with their business.

In that case, you can turn your case around and succeed by showing alternative practices where other employers have been successful in hiring by showing that an alternative practice exists that is equally effective in achieving legitimate employment goals.

The burdens incurred by the employers consist of costs in determining whether the substituted practice is effective. Whether you are an ex-felon or a regular person, you cannot take a lie detector test for employment under any circumstance.

Having been incarcerated or having served time can pose many challenges to your job search and career afterward. A lot of employers rarely hire ex-felons and reject their applications in the review process. If you experience that your employer has biases regarding your employment, you can't do too much. You have to accept this at the end of the day. However, you can try and build your resume properly upon your release to have better employment opportunities.

A few tips and tricks are not to share your history of criminal misconduct unless your employer requires it directly via an application or asks you about it verbally. Don't just give it way; try and give it only when required. Note that you are not bound by law to make every single person aware of your criminal record. However, if you inform your employer right away, you don't have to deal with the rejection later. You can save your energy and apply elsewhere where your employer is not bothered by your record.

Using a professional resume writing service is a great way to make your resume more presentable and access better opportunities. In addition, it will leave a good impression on recruiters and employers. Unfortunately, it can be difficult for a person who's been incarcerated to make an impressive resume, given that they've been off the market for too long.

Note that while making your resume, you should be focused on the future and not what you have done in the past. Explain the experience you have acquired over the few years and discuss what you plan to achieve in the next two, five, or ten years. Show your employer what skillsets make you unique; show them why they should hire you and what an asset you are to the company.

Your resume is not *'one-size-fits-all.'* You're not supposed to apply to different jobs using the same resume over and over again. When you are applying for a job, make sure that your resume is centered on the employer. Do your research on the company before applying and make necessary changes to your resume to make sure it stands out to your employer. Please do your research and use it to your advantage. If the employer finds your resume appealing, they will most likely hire you despite your felony record.

On the subject of resumes, you should know that resumes can be of two types. They are either chronological ones or ones in a functional format. You should consider a functional resume format for your resume to stand out since you are an ex-felon. A functional cv will make your abilities and skills stand out and, at the same time, distract the employer from any specifics about your career, breaks, or gaps that you might have taken.

For example, if you were working while you were incarcerated, instead of saying that you were working for Alabama State Prison, just mention that your work experience includes having worked for the state of Alabama. This kind of labeling is truthful, but it's also accurate, and it can help you get away from a dismissive application from your employer. Make sure that you use advanced vocabulary and a speech style that does not give your prison history away that easily.

Develop a positive attitude. Be aware that revealing any negative information may hurt your job prospects, especially if you have a criminal offense on your record. Stay as true to your personality as possible and make sure that you are honest in your resume; however, refine what you reveal. Try staying focused on your short-term goals instead of divulging them here and there. Remember, *eyes on the prize.* And don't worry about the things that haven't happened yet; worry about crossing the next bridge when you get there.

Make sure that before appearing for an interview, you have googled yourself and your name to see what pops up when you google yourself. Then, get ahead of the game. Your employer would probably want to do the same, so this way, you can anticipate the kind of questions they'll ask and be prepared. Then, while you are in the middle of the research, check and Google what resources employers use to do background checks on employees.

National Felon Friendly Companies

1. Ace Hardware
2. American Airlines
3. Apple, Inc.
4. AT & T
5. Baskin Robins
6. Bed, Bath & Beyond
7. Black & Decker
8. Blue Cross & Blue Shield
9. BP Petroleum
10. Bridgestone
11. Burger King
12. Calvin Klien Inc.
13. Canon
14. Casio
15. Chili's
16. Chipotle
17. Community Education Centres
18. Compaq
19. Dairy Queen
20. Delta Airlines
21. Dollar Tree
22. Domino's Pizza
23. Dunlop Tires
24. Dunkin Donuts
25. Duracell
26. Fujifilm
27. General Electric
28. Goodwill
29. Hilton Hotels
30. Home Depot
31. IBM
32. Mobil Petroleum
33. Motorola
34. Olive Garden
35. Papa Johns
36. PepsiCo
37. PetSmart
38. Pizza Hut
39. Shell Oil
40. Sony
41. Subway
42. Target
43. Toys "R" Us
44. United Airlines
45. US Cellular
46. Verizon
47. Walgreens
48. Wal-Mart
49. Wyndham Hotels
50. Xerox

Public Benefits and Federal Assistance Organizations

The United States is perhaps the largest social welfare nation in the world. Yet, it has the third-highest ranking in per capita social welfare dismemberment throughout the world. It entails the US Government to dispense its people with assistance and amenities. These aids stretch as far as the provision of state-of-the-art healthcare facilities, educational help, housing and accommodation assistance, and monetary funding to those who meet its criteria. The criterion for the qualification of these provisions is and can be insufficient income or poverty.

Your delinquent history may prevent you from receiving many government-aided benefits. However, it doesn't disqualify you from all of the benefits you are entitled to avail as a US Citizen. In addition, if you are convicted of non-drug-related felonies, you'll not be restricted from governmental assistance and aid. Your assistance might have seen a temporary suspension; however, it's not permanent.

Welfare and Food Stamps

The United States provides monetary assistance to its poor, disabled, and senior population through money and food stamps. In addition, several federal programs facilitate families with minor children. However, this program distributes funds differently now due to congress's enactment of the Personal Responsibility and Work Opportunity Reconciliation Act of 1996 (PROWRA).

This program replaced the Assistance to Families with Dependent Children (AFDC) with Temporary Assistance for Needy Families (TANF). A significant difference between TANF and AFDC is that you are bound to receive assistance regardless of your criminal record in TANF. However, the federal government restricts the provision of amenities to families with children. The qualification criteria to meet is that people who receive federal assistance are either employed, seeking employment opportunities, or are being trained for work.

The TANF poses strict restrictions on people who can receive federal assistance and limits them with time. The previous federal assistance program, i.e., the old AFDC program, provided benefits without a time limit. However, a time limit of around five years allows people to seek assistance once in their entire lifetime. Additionally, many IDPs and immigrants are now applicable to receive benefits in light of the new law.

Disability Insurance Benefits

The disability insurance benefits program is a plan that provides monetary assistance to senior citizens, disabled people, and survivors who paid social security to the United States during the span of their life. Having a criminal record doesn't make you ineligible to receive these benefits. However, these benefits are suspended while you are incarcerated. According to the law, if your disability is caused due to your criminal behavior or while you were engaged in a criminal activity that led to your conviction, it cannot be used in deciding whether or not you shall receive federal disability benefits.

Another form of assistance provided by the government toward blind, disabled, and senior citizens is the Supplemental Security Insurance (SSI) program. Eligibility for this program is not affected by a criminal conviction on your hand. However, similar to TANF and food stamps, you are not eligible to receive benefits if you are a fleeing felon or have breached your parole agreement in any way.

State-provided assistance or benefits described earlier are provided by the US Government, so applying for these assistances, you should reach out to social security headquarters to reinstate any benefits that were suspended while you were incarcerated (For disability, old-age, or survivor benefits) or social services office (for TANF or food assistance).

Mental Health and Medical Assistance

Healthcare assistance programs like Medicaid and Medicare are state-run initiatives that provide medical assistance. In particular, these programs, such as Medicaid, provide monetary and material assistance to people who cannot afford to pay for medical or mental health services. Medicare is a healthcare program that partially or fully covers pay for medical and mental health services for senior citizens.

Much like Medicaid, Temporary Assistance for Needy Families is run and managed by the government and is not fully funded. The Medicare program is much similar to Social Security and SSI and is run, managed, and funded by the government.

In the past, Medicaid was operating through the federal welfare program and utilized the same screening process, and applied the same eligibility standards as AFDC and food stamps. As soon as Congress passed the PRWORA, it disassociated Medicaid from monetary assistance and food stamp programs. Consequently, the new standards that the government uses to determine eligibility for monetary assistance and food stamps do not apply to applicants for Medicaid.

Therefore, criminals convicted of drug-related felonies are not declined to receive Medicaid assistance based on their conviction and hence are not bound by any time limit on their health care benefits. In the same way, ex-felons are not denied Medicare if they meet the criteria for qualification despite having a felony charge.

In addition, people who have violated their parole agreement are not disqualified from gaining healthcare assistance by Medicare or Medicaid by the Law. Even though these benefits cannot be availed while imprisoned, you can utilize them on parole or probation.

Public Housing Assistance

The Department of Housing and Urban Development (HUD) administers and provides funding to several government-run and local agencies that provide housing assistance to homeless people or those who need it. This aid comes in the form of cheaper housing in public housing projects, subsidized amounts of private and rental houses, allowances for renters, and monetary assistance to provide support with mortgages and put down cash deposits on houses.

People having criminal records are eligible to receive housing assistance. The federal law doesn't disqualify people from receiving housing assistance because they have a criminal record. However, many housing authorities question or run a background check on people who have a criminal record as part of their screening procedure.

On the flip side, local housing authorities will consider your financial need. They will consider things like your employment status or the employment status of your family members and then deny those with a criminal record. Eviction may follow for individuals and families living in public housing if they are caught in criminal activity while in the apartment or just visiting.

The Supreme Court heavily endorses a zero-tolerance policy toward drug-related offenses in public housing and gives tenants full authority to evict tenants.

Housing Rights

Your criminal record will be dealt with differently when you seek to buy or rent out a house from a private party than when you were applying for public housing, even though the Federal Fair Housing Act prevents both public and private parties from discriminating against potential buyers or renters based on race, religion, nationality, sex or familial sex, or familial status. In addition, the law states that private parties shouldn't base their decision to sell or rent out to you based on their criminal history.

Even though the law doesn't explicitly protect ex-felons from discrimination, that doesn't mean that you are entirely defenseless against discrimination.

First of all, you are under no legal obligation to report your criminal history while applying. Secondly, the law explicitly prevents people from discriminating as applications rejected on criminal convictions can be challenged in court if they are done so with discriminatory intent, especially if they negatively affect one identifiable group of people more than another.

Military Service

The Selective Service Act (the federal law that requires you to register for the draft) states that,

"No person shall be relieved from training and service under this title by reason of conviction of a criminal offense, except where the offense of which he has been convicted may be punished by death or by imprisonment for a term exceeding one year."

Since a felony conviction usually results in a sentence of more than a year, the language of this law suggests that anyone charged with a felony conviction may be exempt from military service. Courts, however, have held otherwise, indicating that the exemption gives rights that are restricted to the government only.

If the draft is over-reinstated, a felony conviction will not in itself exempt you from service.

Reentry Resources for Justice-Involved Individuals

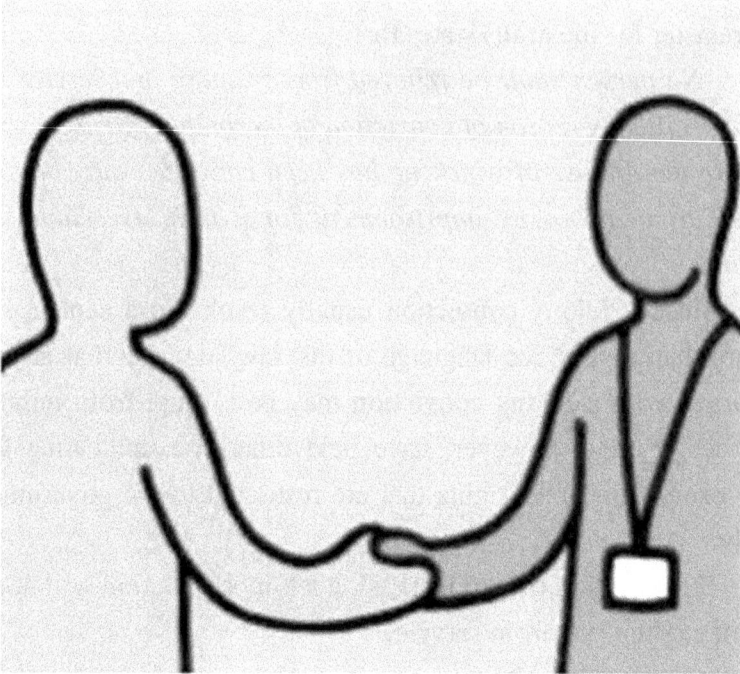

These resources provide information about assistance available on the local level through a state or zip code sort or search.

I am pleased to announce that I, Perrion Roberts, have been selected as one of the ambassadors for United Way 211. United Way's 211 is a robust health and human services referral hotline staffed in partnership with Crisis Services. Sadly, this vital source of help and assistance remains less known among people, which is why I am pleased to help spread the word about it.

211 hotline is perhaps the most comprehensive source of information about local resources and services in the country. Our very own people power it. Thousands of caring, locally trained experts are available to help and guide 24/7. Calls to 211 are confidential and can be anonymous.

The network responds to more than 20 million requests for help every year. 211 can be accessed by phone or computer or the website 211.org.

A toll-free call to 211 connects you to a community resource specialist in your area who can put you in touch with local organizations close to you that provide critical services like:

1. Supplemental food and nutrition programs.
2. Shelter and housing options along with assistance for utilities.
3. Emergency information and disaster relief services.
4. Employment and Educational opportunities.
5. Services for veterans.
6. Provision of health care services, vaccination and health epidemic information.
7. Helps addicts in prevention and rehabilitation programs.

8. Rehabilitation and reentry help for ex-offenders.

9. Support groups for individuals with mental illnesses or special needs.

10. A safe, confidential path out of physical and/or emotional domestic abuse victims.

211 is designed to assist families from all walks of life. Still, most importantly, it benefits the most vulnerable populations, such as the elderly, people with disabilities, and low-income households, by facilitating access to public services.

https://www.211.org/

Alcoholics Anonymous (AA)

https://www.aa.org

American Civil Liberties Union National Prison Project

The National Prison Project is the only organization to litigate on behalf of prisoners at a national level.

733 15th Street NW

Suite 629

Washington, DC 20005

(202) 393-4930

 https://www.aclu.org

American Indian and Alaska Native

The Bureau of Indian Affairs, Financial Assistance, and Social Services, Assistance for Indian Children with Severe Disabilities

https://www.benefits.gov

Benefits.gov

This benefit finder allows you to look for government benefits by category or agency. It links to government information and resources on education, food, housing, disability, Veteran's benefits, and COVID-19,

https://www.benefits.gov

CareerOneStop Job Search Help for Ex-offenders

Sponsored by the Department of Labor, CareerOneStop provides contact information on grograms and government offices by state.

https://www.careeronestop.org

Children's Defense Fund Juvenile Justice Division

25 East Street NW

Washington, DC 20001

(202) 628-8787

https://www.childrensdefense.org

Core Budget Management LLC

Core Budget Management offer credit help to everyone especially returning citizens to improve their credit and help change their lives.

https://www.corebudgetmanagement.com

Ex-offender Assistance Organizations Washington, DC

236 Massachusetts Avenue NE, Suite 505

Washington, DC 20002

E-mail: lacdc@lac-dc.org

Federal Student Aid

There are some restrictions, for instance, those with felony drug possession convictions are not eligible for federal financial aid. Apply anyway. Laws change all the time.

https://www.studentaid.gov

Find Your Local Food Bank, Feeding America

The Feeding America nationwide network of food banks secures and distributes meals through food pantries, meal programs, and mobile services throughout the United States.

Legal Services Alabama

LSA provides FREE civil legal aid to low-income people in all 67 counties in Alabama.

P.O. Box 20787

Montgomery, AL 36120

866-456-4995

legalservicesalabama.org

Narcotics Anonymous

https://www.na.org

National Alliance on Mental Illness (NAMI)

The National Alliance On Mental Illness (NAMI) is an advocacy group for those with family relationships "affected by mental illness." Locate the NAMI affiliate closest to you.

https://wwwnami.org

National Criminal Justice Initiatives Map

Lists re-entry services by state

https://www.nationalreentryresourcecenter.org

National Suicide Prevention Lifeline

The National Suicide Prevention Lifeline
 at 1-800-273-TALK (1-800-273-8255) connects you with a 24-hour crisis center. https://www.suicidepreventionlifeline.org

The National Suicide Prevention Lifeline is now: 988 Suicide and Crisis Lifeline

988 has been designated as the new three-digit dialing code that will route callers to the National Suicide Prevention Lifeline. While some areas may be currently able to connect to the Lifeline by dialing 988, this dialing code will be available to everyone across the United States starting on July 16, 2022.

SCORE

Provides small business mentorship in over 300 U.S. locations. Search by zip code to find an office near you.
https://www.score.org

Substance Abuse and Mental Health Services Administration (SAMHSA) National Helpline

SAMHSA's National Helpline, 1-800-662-Help (4357), is a confidential, free, 24-hours-a-day, 365-days-a-year, information service, in English and Spanish, for individuals and family members facing mental and/or substance use disorders. This service provides referrals to local treatment facilities, support groups, and community-based organizations.
https://www.samhsa.gov

Short-term and Long-term Disability Insurance

Find information about disability services from the usa.gov site, including healthcare coverage, including Medicare and Medicaid. Learn about workplace disability insurance, compensation benefits for disabled veterans, and Social Security benefits for people with disabilities.
https://www.usa.gov

Small Business Administration (SBA) Grants

SBA grants and cooperative agreements information and eligibility. Most grants are made to organizations rather than individuals.
https://www.sba.gov

Salvation Army's Adult Rehabilitation Center

The Salvation Army's Adult Rehabilitation Centers and Harbor Light Programs offer spiritual, emotional, and social assistance. Free programs provide housing, food, counseling, community, and employment.
https://www.centralusa.salvationarmy.org

Social Security Disability

The Social Security and Supplemental Security Income disability programs are the largest of several Federal programs that provide assistance to people with disabilities.
https://www.ssa.gov

Veterans Affairs Disability Compensation

VA disability compensation offers a monthly tax-free payment to Veterans who got sick or injured while serving in the military and to Veterans whose service made an existing condition worse
https://www.va.gov

U.S. Department of Housing and Urban Development (HUD)

451 7th Street S.W., Washington, DC 20410

Phone: (202) 708-1112; TTY: (202) 708-1455 https://www.hud.gov

Youth Reentry

Information for young people leaving juvenile justice residential placement and their family and friends.
https://www.youth.gov

Puzzles and Note Paper

Criminal Thinking Reform Workbook

Name: _____   Date: _____

Criminal Thinking Reform

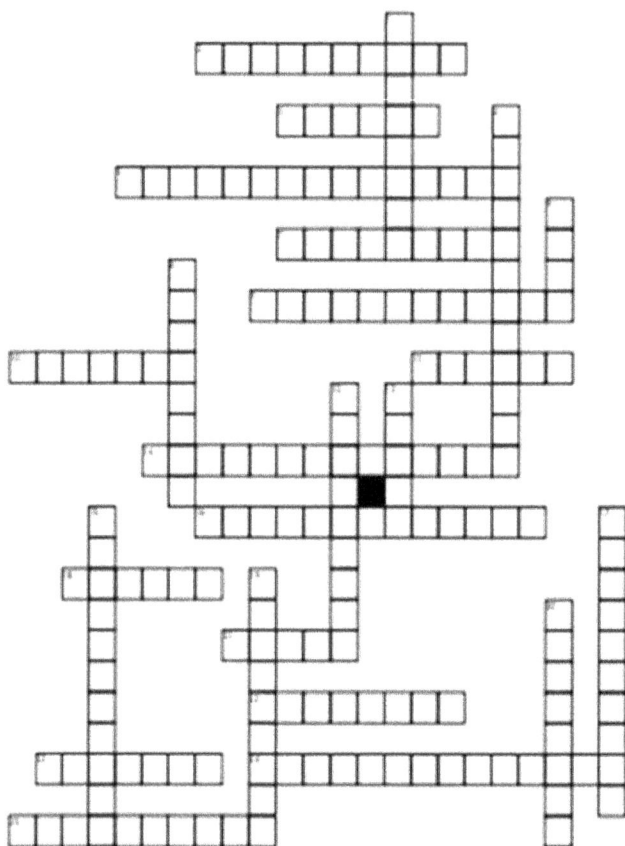

Across

2. The perspective that focuses most heavily on procedural fairness and the rights of the suspects
3. Alibi
5. One specific type of offender that accounts for a vast majority of all offenses
7. The physical part of the crime; the guilty act
9. which type of crime is our biggest
10. Formal process of making a police record of an arrest
11. The first formal police department in the US was created in _____ in 1838
14. A disposition in advance to react in a particular way
16. The purpose of the appellate courts is to

18. After arrest, a defendant will be taken to the police station and
21. Most criminal cases are disposed of by trial
22. In the 1990s crime rates generally
23. Official who runs court and jail security
24. The supreme law of the land is the
25. Radical feminist theory of crimes focus on

Down

1. Guilty Mind
4. Authority vested in a particular court to hear and decide the issues in a particular case decided by location
6. For many decisions, criminal justice officials have at least some discretion
8. Which of the crimes does not fall into the violent crime

12. Problem oriented policing is essentially
13. Conduct in violation of the criminal laws of a state, federal government, or a jurisdiction for which there is no legally acceptable justification or excuse
15. Which theory of crime assumes that person have free will
17. A criminal defense that maintains the police originated the criminal idea or initiated the criminal action.
19. A group of citizens that decides whether there is sufficient evidence to accuse someone of a crime
20. Lower Court

Perrion Roberts

Name: _____ Date: _____

Crime and Consequences

actus reus
arson
assault
causation
concurrence
crime
crime index
crime rate
defense
delinquency
duress
entrapment
harm
insanity
juvenile
larceny
legality
mala prohibita
manslaughter
mens rea
murder
necessity
negligence
nonenforcement
norm
offense
over criminalization
police
punishment
rape
reports
robbery
self·report
status
uniform
victimization

```
Y L O E I D F Y J R E P O R T S Z S A G N A F Y
G V U U V O T C U Y T I S S E C E N K O M E T S
A S M Q K E C Z U N O I T A S U A C I R K L C U
X S A A F M A N S L A U G H T E R T O A R V O T
M E L F G B V Q C M J L E U V O A F X T W R N A
R R A N C F H H Q O I T H U F Z I U T J L L C T
O U P O U B U Q E N A B X F I N B L L X U T U S
N D R I M Z E Z C R A D E L U V U M U R D E R B
P N O T U O B B E Q U N A Y I A N E K P W T R Y
O E H A H R M M U R S N N Y S D T L I X B R E L
L G I Z W A I O L E I E B S F F N I N V N O N Y
I L B I Q R I L U M C L A K L D E N S X O P C H
C I I M C G Y M I R P B J Y A E M E A P N E E T
E G T I E J B R A Y Z U V E U L H V N L E R D F
L E A T S D C L E H X R R Z U I S U I B N F A S
U N L C N R L R J E Z S W D E N I J T V F L U I
L C Q I E P A E D R N C M Z A Q N W Y X O E Y S
R E A V F P P N G E D Q R Q R U U A N R R S W Q
E O O L E X I H M A Y C A D S E P W Z S C R Z G
F J B F D E Y L G Q L R H W O N K K U Q E K M Q
G Y F B M Q U F S P G I Q W N C W T D S M A J S
H H D I E P Z Q W H K M T E H Y C D K I E M M E
W E R P F R W B D I V E U Y O A I I B D N N V G
R C G D G B Y T N E M P A R T N E W S M T Z F B
```

255

About the Author

Perrion Roberts, born June 20, 1964, is a biracial Native American/Black female from Huntsville, AL. She learned the importance of strong work ethics at a young age; Roberts found herself captivated by the idea of becoming a self-made woman early on in life.

While she has worked tirelessly to make her dreams a reality, her path to where she is today has been anything but linear. She was arrested in 2004 for trafficking cocaine and was given a 21-year sentence to be served in Julia Tutwiler Prison for Women.

After being incarcerated for two years, Roberts made parole in 2006 and was offered the blessing of a second chance to turn her life around. She earned her bachelor's degree in Legal Studies from South University and was an inductee of the National Honors Society of Collegiate Scholars.

In 2014, Roberts was granted a full pardon from the State of Alabama and soon after stepped into an advocacy role to help others through the arduous process.

Roberts has been dedicated to her work in Prison Reform, an activist, who supported the lawsuit for restoring ex-felons' voting rights in Alabama, which became law in 2017. Roberts is an active member of the NAACP and an ambassador of the

United Way 211 program. In addition, Roberts has been featured on multiple major television networks and holds a patent for an Automatic Detergent and Fabric Softener Dispenser.

In November 2022, Roberts became the first ever to receive an expungement for her 1992 murder case along with one drug case followed by two other drug cases being dismissed. Roberts has been deemed a trailblazer and a living legend. She continues to fight to break chains for generations to come.

She continues to partner with several other organizations to help others further her cause. Roberts takes pride in the breadth of her achievements, exemplifying firsthand the belief that anything is possible through faith and hard work combined.

"I have used all of the techniques in my book to reform my thinking. I started to see changes in my attitude and behavior, which lead to a more fulfilling life overall. Be blessed and by all means be safe."

- Perrion Roberts

NOTES

www.ingramcontent.com/pod-product-compliance
Lightning Source LLC
Chambersburg PA
CBHW062124020426
42335CB00013B/1085